THOMAS JEFFERSON
Father of Democracy

He was over six feet tall when he was seventeen years old. You would never have thought him handsome, yet his keen gray eyes and alert personality made him attractive to most people. His name was Thomas Jefferson. And if circumstances had prevented this boy from doing his life's work, our own lives today would probably have been very different.

The fact is that much of what we call "the American way of life" was molded in the very beginning by this astonishing man of genius. As author of the Declaration of Independence, as Governor of Virginia, as President and as a citizen in retirement, he fought unceasingly for the basic liberties of our nation.

Here is an exciting account of the stirring and brilliant accomplishments of this great American.

Thomas Jefferson

THOMAS JEFFERSON

Father of Democracy

BY *Vincent Sheean*

ILLUSTRATED BY *Warren Chappell*

RANDOM HOUSE / NEW YORK

Contents

THOMAS JEFFERSON
Father of Democracy

· WILLIAMSBURG

1 · Carrot-Top

HE WAS OVER SIX FEET TALL WHEN HE WAS
seventeen years old—a rather awkward boy, with
carroty red hair and freckles, a pointed nose and
chin. You would never have called him handsome,
and yet his keen gray eyes and generally alert personality made him attractive to most people. He

was fond of horses, music, fox hunting, and ideas in general, with a special leaning toward history and government. His gift for foreign languages, as well as for his native English, was noticeable from his earliest years. His name was Thomas Jefferson, and if anything had happened to keep this boy from living out his life and doing his work, our own lives today would probably have been very different. For the fact is that the greater part of what we call "the American way of life" was molded in the very beginning by this wonderful young man, in his twenties and early thirties, who had one of the most astonishing gifts of genius ever seen in the western world.

He lived a long time—in fact he was eighty-three when he died. This was on the Fourth of July, 1826, the fiftieth anniversary of that Declaration of Independence which he had himself written. His life was useful and interesting to the very end. And even so, if he had died in his middle thirties he still would have been one of the greatest of Americans, author of our civil rights and liberties, of our religious freedom and the basic doctrines of our nation. No other Americans except the noble, serene Washington and the sad and magical Lincoln can be compared to him. The three of them, as different from each other as it is possible to be, were the fathers of the American soul.

Most of what Jefferson believed, wrote, said and did could have been imagined from a study of his character at the age of seventeen. That is, his whole life was consistent and harmonious. He did not change his mind every week or so: all the main lines were there from the beginning to the end. He learned much as he grew older, because his interests were wide and his curiosity endless. He cared about building and designing things, creating things, investigating things. He was always on the lookout for a new idea in farming or bookkeeping or carpentry, a new kind of clock or wagon or stove, new horizons and frontiers for his young country. But most of what he learned as he grew older was simply information. What he had in him from the beginning was the principle of what he called "human rights," which nowadays, for all practical purposes, is what we call "civil rights." That we have these rights today is owing chiefly to him.

Young Jefferson went to William and Mary

College at Williamsburg, in Virginia. This was the capital of the colony (the "Old Dominion" they called it) in those days. It had a British Governor and a legislative assembly of Virginians elected by the freemen of the colony. The British Governor maintained a certain amount of stately routine, as representative of the King, and the Assembly was always the excuse for a number of parties, dances or "routs" as they were called, and endless private gatherings in the rooms of the Raleigh Tavern or the houses of the little town. If you go to Williamsburg today you can see it all, carefully reconstructed according to the old records and pictures, and you will realize that although it was small and provincial—not at all like London or Paris or even the New York of that time—it had its own dignity and formality.

For the Virginians were inclined to be a rather formal people. The colony was agricultural, not industrial or commercial. In those big country houses where all of Jefferson's friends lived there was a sincere regard for the pleasanter and more graceful customs of the old world. True, this existed on a basis of slavery, which had been introduced to the colony by Englishmen and Bostonians about a hundred years before. Against slavery Jefferson was to raise his voice in vain throughout his long life. One of his main grievances against the English always was that they had brought slavery into the southern states and particularly into his beloved Virginia. He tried to get something to this effect into his most famous work, the Declaration of Independence, but it was cut out because in addition to the natural Southern objections, other Congressmen feared that it would offend the Massachusetts people who were just as responsible as the English for this evil.

The Virginians who went to Williamsburg for the Assembly, or who were educated at William and Mary College, were chiefly what is called "aristocrats," which is to say landowners proud of their ancestors and their acres. They all owned slaves and most of the boys took slaves to college with them, just as they took their horses. As a matter of fact the Virginians were by no means of "aristocratic" origin in the old country. Most of them came from the small farmer and merchant classes. There were, however, enough "Cavaliers" amongst them to give a tone of dashing romanticism to all the rest, and after a few generations in the colony everybody was a "Cavalier." The art of flourishing a plumed hat and making a court bow was encouraged as much at Williamsburg as in London. No Virginia gentleman went to an evening party without either a powdered wig or a thorough job of powdering on his own hair.

Thomas Jefferson's mother was a Randolph, which is to say a member of the most powerful land-owning family in Virginia. His father was of yeoman stock (small farmer, that is), and the mixture of the two strains might account for some of Jefferson's lifelong impatience with the claims of the so-called "aristocracy." He always regarded the concentration on ancestry as being downright silly, and dismisses it with some scorn in his Autobiography.

But it must have been an advantage, just the same, for a boy growing up in the Virginia of those days, to know that he was by birth entitled to dispute on equal terms with anybody else in the whole neighborhood. Jefferson loved to argue, to discuss, to work out ideas in conversation. If he had not had the advantages of ancestry and property, he might not have found it so easy to do so, especially in his first youth. That was a class-conscious society, based on slavery as we have noticed, and we are all of us very lucky that Jefferson did not have to worry about such things in his formative years. Our greatest democratic-republican "radical," as they called him, was able to impose his advanced and modern ideas upon an entrenched landed aristocracy not only because of his own powers of persuasion, but also because he was one of them himself. Whatever he said or did, they could neither disown nor disregard him.

Thomas Jefferson's father, Peter, died when the boy was fourteen years old, and from that time onward Thomas was the head of the family, owner of the property, and responsible for the welfare of his mother, sister and others. This may have made him grow up a little more quickly and accept responsibility a little sooner than usual. He had gone to English school at five and Latin school at nine. His last two years before college were spent under the tuition of James Maury, a Whig clergyman whom he remembered to the end of his days with affection. At sixteen he went to William and Mary College.

Our knowledge of his first year at college is not extensive, but by the time he was seventeen, in his second year, we learn that he was already a friend of some older men of great distinction and interest. He owed this not only to his lively conversation and manners, but also to his talent for playing the violin. The British Governor of those days, Fauquier, liked music and wanted to play trios and quartets with anybody who was able to do so. One of the volunteers was the leading lawyer of the town and whole colony, George Wythe, a man who was to play a great part in Jefferson's life. Thus we see young Tom, the carrot-head, at the age of seventeen, playing classical music with dignitaries more than twice his age, at the Palace of the Governor. There can be no doubt that the conversation of men like Fauquier and Wythe, who knew the great world of London and Paris, who were cultivated in literature and all the arts, had a great effect on the awkward boy from Albemarle County.

Tom was an excellent student, particularly in

Often Jefferson played in a violin trio at the Palace.

languages and history, but he liked to have a good time too. He was wide awake to the charms of the girls from the time he went to college, and there is plenty of evidence to show that they also liked him. He loved dancing, he was bright and gay and sometimes foolish, and he could ride a horse as well as anybody in Virginia. These characteristics more than recompensed for his great height, awkwardness and lack of regular good looks. One of his great "flirts" at Williamsburg was a girl whom he called "Belinda," in accordance with the romantic customs of the period. (Everybody had to be given some special name that was not her own.) This young lady afterwards married somebody else and lived happily ever after, but young Tom Jefferson moaned and groaned about her for about a year and a half of his college time. From the tone of his letters to his friends, some of which have been preserved, we get the idea that he was thoroughly enjoying himself by pretending a hopeless passion.

His great friend in college was a talented young man named Dabney Carr, with whom he could read poetry, ride horses and talk about life. Dabney

Carr was immensely important to Jefferson and, although he died young, was never forgotten. He is buried at Monticello beside Jefferson. The site for Monticello, in fact, Jefferson's own house which he spent twenty-five years building, was picked out by the two of them when they were seventeen. Tom and Dabney used to go there and lie under the trees on the top of the hill and read poetry or discuss politics. They took a vow that whichever one died first, the other would see that he was buried somewhere on that hill. Even then, at seventeen or eighteen, the wooded hill seemed to Jefferson the place above all others where he wanted to build his own house in his own way and live in peace.

William and Mary College gave a "classical" education, with much emphasis on Greek and Latin. These languages, as well as French, Jefferson mastered during his years at college. Later on he taught himself Italian, Spanish and old Anglo-Saxon, sometimes without knowing exactly how they ought to be pronounced. In later years when some Italians came to Monticello they found that Jefferson knew their language perfectly well, understood it when they spoke, but had no practice in saying it aloud himself.

The red-haired boy who played quartets at the Governor's Palace must have been quite a surprise to those who met him then. In the first place, although he was a landed proprietor from the age of fourteen—his father left him 1,900 acres—and a slave owner as well, with an ample pedigree on his mother's side of the house, he was never at any time in agreement with the aristocratic point of view in Virginia. His father was a yeoman, and Albemarle County, where they lived, was in those days practically a frontier. The Virginia "aristocrats," many of them Jefferson's relatives, lived lower down toward the sea, along the James River. They thought the people from the higher lands farther west were what nowadays would be called hillbillies, uncouth and scarcely housebroken.

Virginia was immense—the biggest and richest of all the colonies—including all of what are now the states of West Virginia, Kentucky, Ohio, Illinois, Indiana, Michigan and Wisconsin. Most of the vast country to the west was unsettled as yet, and the aristocrats of tidewater Virginia had no desire to go there. Jefferson, on the other hand, grew up in the hill country facing the west, and the Blue Ridge Mountains had far more to do with forming his imagination than the James River. He looked to the west, and was indeed the American who saw most clearly, in those days, the scope of our western destiny.

So, when he met with his eastern friends and relatives at Williamsburg, although he was never at any time quarrelsome, he certainly felt the difference between his own point of view and theirs. They believed in a kind of feudal system.

Yet he, an eldest son inheriting an entailed estate, was in fact the man who broke up the feudal system and made it possible for all children, including girls, to inherit equally. He did this quite a few years after his college days, but we possess the evidence that even as a boy in college he had those ideas. He came down to Williamsburg as a believer in democracy, a frontiersman at seventeen, naturally and instinctively sure that men are and "of right ought to be" free and equal. In some ways his beliefs grew more fixed as he grew older, but there is no doubt that they were in him from the beginning.

This set him off from his fellows, but it seems to be true that he never got into real personal quarrels over such matters. He could argue by the hour, but his good nature and friendly disposition were such that he seems to have been popular all along, early and late. It is remarkable that with all his love of parties, fox hunts, music and singing and dancing, he never took up either cards or tobacco. Williamsburg was a small capital, but it was greatly given to the gayeties (or vices) associated with great cities. Thus Francis Fauquier, the British Governor at whose table Jefferson was frequently a guest, had a passion for gambling, as was quite usual in those days. It was customary for the men to drink heavily and play cards for large stakes. Tobacco was used in all sorts of ways—to smoke, to chew, to snuff. Jefferson acquired and kept throughout his life a love of good wine, but gambling did not appeal to him and it seems that he never learned any card games. Much as he liked horses, he could frequent the races without gambling on them. And al-

though later on tobacco was one of his main crops at Monticello—most of the furniture and other valuables from London and Paris were bought by the tobacco crop—Jefferson himself never used it.

We get the idea, therefore, that although the young man enjoyed life thoroughly and was as sociable and high-spirited as anybody else in college, he had some deeply rooted common sense or seriousness of purpose which kept him out of harm's way. He must have had this fundamental seriousness beneath all the fun because in fact he did a great deal of work. His standing as a student was always high, and the older men who took an interest in him were men of real scholarship and distinction. George Wythe, the eminent lawyer who had so great an influence over him, would not have bothered if he had not felt in this lively, red-haired young fellow the promise of talent and fulfilment.

And it was Wythe who determined Jefferson's choice of a profession. No doubt they had long talks about it. It would have been quite easy for Jefferson to live the life of a country squire, taking care of his acres and his slaves, without any attempt to learn more after his twentieth year. But his natural bent toward history and government made him want to learn the law, to become a lawyer. And in his older friend, George Wythe, he saw the wisest and most accomplished lawyer of the colony. Therefore when he left college he settled down to a long stretch of hard work, "reading law," as they said, in the offices of George Wythe.

2 · *The Young Lawyer*

YOU COULD "READ LAW" IN A VARIETY OF WAYS
then. There were no law schools at the universities
and the system of examinations for admission to
the bar was rather loose. You studied in the offices
of a lawyer, you mastered Coke and all the other
authorities on English legal practice, and when you
were ready (or thought you were ready) you applied for your examination. Some young men did

this after very little preparation and were admitted just the same. Patrick Henry, the orator who swept all audiences off their feet, passed his bar examinations after only three months of study. He was able to do so because, by all accounts, his style in speech-making was so fiery and impressive that minor defects (such as book knowledge) did not count.

Thomas Jefferson took five years at it. He was thorough by nature, and there is no doubt that he wanted to learn everything he could. (This was so to his extreme old age.) But perhaps he might have worked a little less and learned a little less if he had had, like Patrick Henry, the special gift of oratory. This he did not possess. His voice was not strong or beautiful, he relied much more on reason than on emotion, and he seldom tried to use eloquence as a weapon. He believed that men are convinced by reason and reflection, not by argument, and a person who believes in this way is very unlikely to have much power as an orator.

And yet, by the way, Jefferson's own speeches when we read them today are far more impressive than the oratorical flights of Patrick Henry. Henry was probably one of those men who must be heard and seen: his written works give us no idea of the thrilling effect he made on his contemporaries. "Give me liberty or give me death," his greatest speech, although it can still move us when we remember the circumstances, does not actually compare with either one of Jefferson's inaugural addresses in power of thought.

Jefferson as a law student and afterwards as a lawyer always relied on hard work, close reasoning and exact expression. Such qualities look fine in print. They stand the test of time. They are as valuable today as they were a hundred and seventy or eighty years ago. But in the rough-and-tumble of a court trial or a congressional debate they do not make that immediate effect which is required. Perhaps this is why Jefferson became more and more inclined to use his pen rather than his voice— to make no speeches at all unless they were absolutely necessary—and to rely, most of all, upon the permanent rather than the temporary effect. For he was, of course, a very great writer, one of the greatest in his own field that modern times have produced. In these matters, writing and speaking, he seems to have a kinship with Abe. Lincoln, whose voice was also as weak as his pen was mighty.

Young Jefferson worked very hard at his law studies, and his habit of keeping notes and journals started at that time or even earlier. He seems to have felt, as many others have before and after him, that to write a thing down is one fairly sure way to remember it. (And if you forget it, the note is always there to remind you.)

Sometimes it is hard to understand how a man as busy as Jefferson was from his twenties onward could possibly have written so much. There are twenty big volumes in his collected writings as put out in the Memorial Edition, and we may be sure that a good deal of what he wrote has been lost. He must have made himself write notes, journals, letters and innumerable other things (including private essays to clarify his own thought) for several hours every day of his life. To get the thinking on paper was probably one of his aids to thought: he could then tear it up and start over. But he certainly did try, right from the beginning, to express himself as clearly as possible, in the best language he could find for his purpose. He never seems to have striven for showy effects of language, but merely for the most exact, strong and clear utterance of his thought.

This note-taking and constant writing flourished during the five years that Jefferson studied law, and it was a good thing for the United States that this was so. It gave him such practice in strong, clear statement that when his pen was needed for his country's service he was able to respond with assurance.

A great deal of what Jefferson wrote down during these law-student years went into what he called his *Commonplace Book*, which for a long time he thought burned up in the fire at his mother's house. The *Commonplace Book* was afterwards found and can be seen today in the Congressional Library as evidence of the great care and industry that went into his apprentice years.

He did not stay in Williamsburg all this time, of course. His mother's house at Shadwell in Albemarle County was also his own, and he and his friend Dabney Carr, still his best friend and fellow student at Wythe's law chambers, often went there. Jefferson worked just the same whether he was in Williamsburg or at home or anywhere else. He had a regular daily routine which would make most of us cringe to contemplate. He rose very early and read scientific subjects until eight o'clock. (These included zoölogy, botany, agriculture, chemistry and others.) From eight to twelve, according to his own outline of studies, he gave his whole time to reading law and nothing but law. From twelve to one he recommended the reading of politics. (And, knowing Jefferson, we can be sure he followed his own recommendation.) During the afternoon the student read history, and between dinner and bedtime he read literature.

He and his friend Carr probably carried out this program most of the time, but it could not have been invariable because they were both still fond of dancing parties, pretty girls and highly bred horses. Jefferson's agitation over the Virginia belle he calls "Belinda" was at its height during the first year and a half of his law studies, so we must assume that he had a little time not given to serious reading.

And then, too, there was excitement in the air at

Williamsburg. The American Revolution, which was not an event, not a plot and not a plan, but a sort of natural and inevitable growth, was in its earliest stages. Nobody in Williamsburg foresaw then, so far as we know, that this was to be the birth of a new nation. But the year was 1763 and Jefferson was twenty years old. (He was born April 13th, 1743.) He took the liveliest interest in the debates then going on about the conflicting rights and privileges of the King in London and the thirteen colonies in America.

The King was George III, who seems to have been one of the stupidest men who ever interfered with the affairs of nations. He was constantly insisting on his rights and privileges, having been encouraged to do so by his domineering mother, and probably dreamed of bringing back the days when the King's will was law in England and throughout his empire. In any case, so far as the Americans were concerned he stood very nearly alone, and by sheer pigheaded obstinacy succeeded at last in driving the colonists into rebellion. All the best minds in England were against the King's wishes in this matter, and even his own cabinet ministers carried out his plans with reluctance and misgiving. The finest orators of the House of Commons, Chatham and Burke, the leaders of the opposition, took the side of the Americans, and the masses of the English people never even realized what was going on until it was too late to remedy matters.

For the colonists in America were not in the least disloyal to the King. They were claiming, in fact, merely the rights of freeborn Englishmen, the same rights held by their relatives in the old country. Beyond a doubt they had already become a different breed, owing to generations of life in this immense new country, but they did not know it. Besides, their rising mercantile interests needed freedom. These colonists thought of themselves as Englishmen. They called this country "British America." They did not in the least want to rebel against the King, and all through the early years of the revolutionary movement they kept on sending him solemn addresses of loyalty. For a long time they pretended that it was the King's ministers, not the King himself, who were infringing their rights (even though a good many of them knew better).

One dispute after another arose between the thirteen colonies and the government of their mother country. The truth of the matter probably was that the men who lived in the new states between Massachusetts and Georgia had more or less grown up. They had come of age. They were ready to govern themselves and were actually doing so by means of their colonial assemblies in most matters. Each colony was a separate political organism. Except for Franklin's "Albany Plan" in 1754, no union had been suggested. Yet there was a current of feeling and sympathy running through them all. As we look back on it now we can see that the American Revolution was such a natural development that it probably would have happened even if George III had not provided the reasons. It might have been a little slower in taking place, but it was bound to happen sometime. London was entirely too far off in those days to exercise any real control over the new generations in this enormous country.

And, moreover, the colonists had already fought the French and the Indians in a series of wars and acquitted themselves well. They thought they had won these wars, so far as this part of the world was concerned. And they also thought they were well able to take care of themselves without any protective British troops or garrisons.

The King thought differently. He wanted to keep garrisons at stated points in the colonies, and he wanted the colonies to contribute to the support of those garrisons. He also distrusted the tendencies towards independent thinking, undue liberalism and self-assertion on the part of the American territories. One of his earliest mistakes in this regard was an attempt to force the colony of Virginia to pay the clergy of the Established Church (that is, the Church of England) at a higher rate than the Virginia Assembly permitted.

These forgotten quarrels sometimes seem a little funny today. The fact is that the clergymen of the Established Church received their pay from the colony of Virginia in the form of tobacco. The Virginia Assembly, no doubt with a certain amount of anti-Church feeling in the air, voted a law called the Two Penny Act which said that the clergy's salaries would henceforth be paid in money calculated at the rate of twopence for each pound of tobacco. That was a very low rate, and amounted to cutting down the clergy's pay to far less than they were used to receiving. The turmoil was considerable. The Bishop of London had Virginia in his diocese, and he aroused the clergy of England to indignation. The King's Privy Council then ruled that the clergy in Virginia must be paid at the regular market rate for tobacco—far above twopence a pound. This, of course, was overruling the elected Assembly of Virginia, which already had grown to think of itself as self-governing.

In just that year when Jefferson began to study law in Williamsburg, a parson from Hanover, Virginia, brought suit against the colony to get his salary (sixteen thousand pounds of tobacco) in money at the regular market price, in accordance with the King's decision. The parson was Jefferson's old tutor, Maury. The court ruled that the parson could get his money but the exact sum must be decided by a jury trial.

So began one of the great early episodes of the

Revolution. Among other things, it introduced Jefferson to Patrick Henry, the impassioned orator, who descended on Williamsburg to argue the case against the parson. Feeling was wildly excited in the town, and Patrick Henry made one of his most flamboyant speeches, full of fire and brimstone. As a result the jury gave the parson the smallest possible damages, a mob collected to carry Patrick Henry in triumph from the courtroom, and another step had been taken towards the eventual independence of the colonies.

Jefferson met Patrick Henry at this time and was greatly impressed—so much so that he used to entertain Henry whenever he came to Williamsburg. They were not in the least similar, and it is beyond doubt that later on Jefferson's admiration was somewhat modified, but at that time, to a boy of twenty who had probably never seen a "patriot" before, the weird and violent speechmaker was something new and wonderful.

A "patriot"—and the word was quite new then in the colonies—was defined as a person whose first loyalty was to the land of his birth. It was for some years regarded as being radical and disloyal to be a "patriot," and those loyal to the King (the Tories) had no worse term of abuse. Eventually the word became a badge of honor claimed by almost everybody, but in the early years of the revolutionary period it was just the reverse. Only a very bold and brave man would claim to be a "patriot" for his own native Virginia rather than for the mother country he had never seen.

It was this boldness and bravery that attracted Jefferson to Patrick Henry. The famous orator was unknown at that time (1763). He was just twenty-seven years old, seven years Jefferson's senior, and had been practicing law in relative obscurity for three years only. He had first failed as a farmer and as a businessman (storekeeper) in his native Hanover County, and then became a lawyer on a mere three months' preparation, as we have seen. His fiery speech in the case of the parson's suit against the colony made him an idol in Virginia, and he remained one of the most popular of all figures for the rest of his life. He did not have the education, the polish or the manners of the tidewater aristocrats, and this, too, helped to make him adored by the common people. As years went on he calmed down a good deal, and indeed ended his life on the opposite side of the fence from Jefferson—as a staunch supporter of conservatism and privilege—but in these early years he was all flame and fury. Most men in Williamsburg were startled by him at first, and it took the conservatives a long time to get used to his electrical excitement, but the ordinary people were never able to resist his splendid voice and flashing eyes. Whether he combed his hair or not did not matter to them.

But it took a good deal more than one backwoods orator to teach George III a lesson. As a means of re-asserting the authority he felt he was losing in the colonies, and to make the colonists pay for the British garrisons he was sending among them, the King's ministers put through a bill called the Stamp Act, which would impose a tax on every legal paper devised in America. This applied to wills, marriages, contracts and everything else requiring legal record. The tax was on a sliding scale, and went all the way from about six cents to fifty dollars (threepence to ten pounds).

The Stamp Act passed the House of Commons without arousing much interest. But when the news was heard in America there was a tempest of indignation. What? Have taxes imposed from overseas? Pay for a garrison nobody wanted or needed? Surrender the colonial assembly's right to levy its own taxes? So ran the arguments. "We are freeborn Englishmen, even if born in America," was the usual way of putting it. "We claim the same rights as Englishmen born in England. They can't be taxed unless they do it themselves. Neither can we."

At twenty-one and twenty-two years of age, then, Jefferson was already plunged into the kind of political discussion that was to fill so much of his life. His master in the law, George Wythe, was an urbane and cultivated man whose natural bent, in other times, might have been conservative, but in these matters his heart was with the colonies. Wythe was an enormous influence upon Jefferson then, as he was upon so many young men who studied law in his offices (John Marshall, the great Chief Justice of later years, was one of them too).

Wythe was very slow to entertain any ideas of independence or rebellion, but when those ideas were forced upon him ten years later, and when his pupil Jefferson produced the Declaration of Independence, Wythe went the limit to support the making of a new nation. Those ten years in Wythe's life and thinking were a parallel to what was going on all over the thirteen colonies. The colonists started the ten years as loyal Englishmen demanding the rights of all other Englishmen; they ended the ten years proclaiming themselves to be Americans, free and independent.

Patrick Henry came to the fore again over the Stamp Act. He was elected to the Virginia Assembly in 1765 and came again to Williamsburg like a cyclone, determined to say his say. Most of the older men—Wythe included—were afraid of him, as probably most of us would be today. Jefferson still thought he was a strange and wonderful man and gave him house room, as usual. In the streets of the little town Jefferson, the red-haired gangly-shanks of twenty-two, might have been seen ambling along beside his famous friend, whose personality was already so well known that everybody in the place spoke or bowed to him.

On the Stamp Act Patrick Henry made one of his most famous speeches. The Virginia Assembly

was in a majority against the new taxation, as were
the other colonial assemblies, but men were not
yet ready for the kind of language Patrick Henry
used. One passage in his great speech against the
Stamp Act has been familiar for generations.
"Caesar had his Brutus," the orator declared,
"Charles I his Cromwell, and George III"—here
he was interrupted by cries of "Treason!" One of
those who cried "Treason!" was George Wythe.
Patrick Henry went on: "George III may profit by
their example! If this be treason, make the most
of it."

Henry's great speech was made in support of
what were called the Virginia Resolutions, a set of
statements resisting the Stamp Act and asserting
the right of the colonial assemblies to make laws
for themselves. True, they had been doing so for
years, but it never had been clearly established that
this was their right and that the parliament in the
mother country could not make laws for them. The
British Constitution grew up by custom and never
has been given written form as a whole, even today. Consequently the border line between what
the colonies could or could not do what the home

*"If this be treason," shouted Henry,
"make the most of it."*

parliament could or could not do, was indistinct, and there was room for plenty of argument. The argument was to express itself during the next ten years in a steady progress towards independence from the old country—which meant, when it came to the final crisis, revolution and war.

To the young man ploughing his way through the law books in George Wythe's office every stage of the development was to prove passionately interesting. He had a natural liking for government, politics, law and history, and he was reaching his young manhood in a period when, by the force of events, these things concerned everybody deeply. He could hardly have seen or met anybody in those days in Williamsburg who did not discuss, with more or less heat and light, the ruling topics of the day.

And yet, as happens often in these great, slow movements involving millions of people, the flare-up of passion over the Stamp Act died down for a while afterwards, for a period of two or three years. Young Jefferson had been present when his friend Patrick Henry made the dramatic speech ending with "If this be treason make the most of it." He tells us that he stood in the doorway between the lobby and the floor of the Assembly, listening and looking with all his might. The excitement at the time was tremendous and he felt it to the full. He was amazed, thinking back over it later, that such patriotic ardor should have been followed, as he said, by "a state of insensibility and inaction." King George III had been more or less forced by his own ministers to repeal the Stamp Act because the American resistance to it was "bad for business" in England. He did not, however, give up his idea that his government had a right to tax the colonies without consulting their legislatures, and he was supported by a small but important group of Tory die-hards who were much heard in the debate. Virginia and all the other colonies continued to feel uneasy, but for the moment there was a lull in public events.

During this lull Jefferson finished his law studies, passed his bar examination and set up practice as a lawyer in Williamsburg (1767). He practiced law for seven years, from then until 1774, and was forced to give it up only because his increasing political work—with the Revolution at hand—gave him no more time for it. His average earnings at his profession during these seven years were about $1,500 a year (300 English pounds) which, with all the values of money taken into consideration, would have been equal to $15,000 today, if not more. For a young lawyer such earnings were considerable, and it is clear that he was a success in his profession. He did not need the money—he could have lived well without it—but it shows us that he was highly regarded in the time and place.

His success was not due to special gifts of speech making, either: it came most of all from careful preparation and very sound legal argument, based on his thorough studies. When we look over the cases he took and argued during his seven years at the bar, a few stand out as characteristic of his lifelong interest in what he called "human rights." There was, for instance, one called "Howell versus Netherland," which brought out his passionate dislike for slavery and his desire to curb it in any way possible.

The case was argued in 1770 but dealt with events beginning in 1705. In that year—sixty-five years before—a white woman had given birth to a child by a Negro father. According to the law of the time, this woman was sentenced to slavery until she was thirty-one years old. While she was a slave she had a daughter, and years later this daughter gave birth to a son. The child was sold into slavery by the owner of grandmother and mother. The new owner claimed that this little boy, the grandson, was his slave until the age of thirty-one.

Jefferson took the case. He had to admit that the law compelled the grandmother and the daughter to be slaves for the stated number of years, but he argued that this slavery could not be extended to the grandson or "other issue more remote."

In arguing this point of view, Jefferson even then (at 27 years of age) brought forth the ideas that were to govern his whole life. He spoke for "the law of nature," under which he said all men are born free; he spoke for "human rights" and "natural liberty."

The court was shocked to hear anybody argue that Negroes had such rights, or that there was anything wrong or false about enslaving them. Jefferson lost the case—in fact the court did not even wish to hear the other side argued. Jefferson's own doctrine had lost the case for him, and the child went into slavery.

Even now, so early in his public life, Jefferson was not afraid to declare what he most firmly believed. Since Virginia was based on slavery, it was not popular doctrine—and since Jefferson himself was a slave owner from birth, his fellow Virginians were shocked to hear him argue against them.

He did, however, get about a hundred cases a year during the time he was practicing law, and there could hardly have been any other lawyer his age who did so well. In spite of that fact he did not much like practice, and once he abandoned it he never returned. In fact he held rather a poor opinion of lawyers in general, "whose trade it is," he said, "to question everything, yield nothing and talk by the hour."

His natural leaning toward politics made him an obvious candidate for the Assembly as soon as he was old enough. He had become a squire and justice of the peace when he was 21, since the family property was his. By the time he was twenty-six and practicing law he was ready to become a member of the Virginia House of Burgesses, and his friends and neighbors of Albemarle County were more than ready to elect him. He held open house for them at Shadwell, his mother's family estate where he then lived, and they acclaimed him as their natural candidate.

In all this activity, both in the law and in the House of Burgesses to which he was now going, Jefferson's constant companion was Dabney Carr, brilliant speaker and great young talent, who had already married his friend's sister Martha and looked forward to a sort of parallel career with Jefferson. They never gave up their habit of going to the "little mountain," Monticello, where Jefferson had already begun to build that house which was his lifelong dream and is today one of the most beautiful in America.

In the House of Burgesses, too, the red-haired young man made haste to put forth his views on human rights. One of the very first efforts he made in politics was to write and introduce a law which would have given slave owners the right to set their slaves free ("emancipate" them) if they desired to do so. No doubt this arose from his own feeling that he ought not to own slaves, since he detested slavery; and yet under Virginia law he could not set his slaves free no matter how much he might want to do so. It was "dangerous."

And the other members of the Assembly, all slave owners themselves, showed how "dangerous" they thought it was by defeating Jefferson's first effort. This failure did not discourage him, and whenever he could strike a blow at slavery he did so to the end of his days.

No young man of Jefferson's wit, talent, gayety and good nature could fail to be popular with the ladies, especially when his other advantages (wealth and great family connections) were added. There are plenty of stories about his flirtations in early years, but nobody knows how serious they were. What we know is that along about this time, as he was coming to his maturity in the work of his life, law and politics, he made the acquaintance of a charming young widow, Mrs. Bathurst Skelton, born Martha Wayles. Her father, John Wayles, was a lawyer of great success, owner of an estate called "The Forest" in Charles City County, and is described by Jefferson himself as "a most agreeable companion."

Martha Wayles had married Bathurst Skelton,

Often Martha played on the harpsichord for Jefferson.

who died very soon after the marriage, and she was in fact only twenty-three when she married Jefferson. She had beauty, grace and charm, and she shared Jefferson's devotion to music. From their first acquaintance they played duets together, he on the violin and she at the harpsichord, and they also sang together to her accompaniment. Jefferson made his way to "The Forest" as often as he could—so did many other young men of the colony—and by the time he was twenty-nine the prize was his. He and his Martha were married from her father's house on New Year's Day, 1772. And before very long there were three Martha Jeffersons: his wife, his sister (Mrs. Dabney Carr) and his daughter.

All of the elements of a happy life in the time and place were brought together for Jefferson during these years. He was busy and successful in his own right; he had an inherited estate and house and slaves; he was a man of mark in politics and public life well before he was thirty. With all this he had that mountain he loved, Monticello, and was making progress with building his great house there. One part of the main house was in fact completed before his marriage and he took his bride there—through a blinding snowstorm over very bad roads—on their wedding day. His happiness with Martha is beyond doubt, and although she added greatly to the Jefferson estate through her inheritance, there is no ground for believing that he "married for money." It was an accusation made in later years when his political enemies were ready to say anything about him.

There were some sorrows, of course. No life is without them. For one thing, Jefferson was extremely fond of books and had built up a library of nearly three thousand volumes at Shadwell, his birthplace. That house burned down one spring day in 1770, and with it all his books. He mourned the books more than the house. (According to an old story, his slaves saved his violin but no books.)

And then, too, Dabney Carr, the greatest friend he ever had, died not long after his marriage. Jefferson was absent at the time, as he had been when Shadwell burned. The family buried Dabney there, but when Jefferson came home he had the body disinterred and taken to Monticello, in accordance with the pledge they had made to each other as boys. It lies there now, along with Jefferson himself and his family. Dabney left his widow—Jefferson's sister Martha—with six small children, all of whom were taken into the house at Monticello and brought up with Jefferson's own daughters.

But all of these events of his personal life, good and bad, happy and sorrowful, were soon to be overshadowed by an immense and absorbing public task. Young as he was, Thomas Jefferson was already a leader for his fellow Virginians. He was now about to become the principal spokesman for the doctrine of American freedom—the "pen of the Revolution" as has been said—and thus not only a creator (with others) of the new nation, but author of the *reason why* such things should be. He never ceased to be devoted to his family. Many and many a time he tried to get out of public life altogether so as to give his whole time to them and to his beloved house. But from now on he never really could lead a private life. He merged with the nation, belonged to the nation, and what arouses our incessant interest and astonishment is how much he was able, one man alone, to do for this country and its whole development from then to now. We owe our rights and liberties to many great and good men of the past, but most of all to him, at the very beginning of our time as a nation on this earth.

3 · *The Pen of the Revolution*

GEORGE III AND HIS TORY MINISTERS NEVER
had given up their belief that they had the right
to tax the American colonies without the consent of
the colonial legislatures. They had repealed the
Stamp Act for business reasons. Now, after the
lull was over, a Tory named Charles Townshend
introduced into the House of Commons a bill

taxing the Americans on glass, white and red lead, tea and paper, among other things. All of these were imports, not then obtainable except from England.

Young Jefferson came into his political life as a representative just when this new assertion of the King's claim was made. In addition to the taxes in the Townshend Act, another law from London declared that Americans charged with political (and some other) offenses could not be tried by their own courts and juries, but must be sent to England for trial.

All the colonies were in an uproar. Up in Massachusetts the "patriots," as they were now increasingly called, had the leadership of a tough citizen, Samuel Adams, who was not inclined to give in on any point. He was for a long time ahead of the other colonial leaders in his determination to resist and in his ability to influence the people of his own colony, particularly the young men of Boston.

In Virginia there were equally determined men, perhaps younger and certainly all of a different kind (landowners, slave owners mostly). Jefferson, Patrick Henry and Richard Henry Lee were among them. George Washington, the calm man, was slow to get excited on any question, but soon he was to be on their side.

The King knew very little about America and his ministers hardly more. To them, as to the colonists, it seems to have been largely a question of principle, and they do not seem to have realized in London that principles could be so important.

Young Jefferson and his friend Dabney Carr (then still alive) took part in numerous private meetings to debate all this with the older men of the Assembly. There were Richard Henry Lee and Francis Lightfoot Lee among them: they were all themselves "aristocrats" but not Tories. The landowning aristocracy of Virginia at first was not with them—regarded them as black sheep—and preferred to conduct the debate with London on a basis of strict loyalty to the King. But these "forward men," as they were called, had already perceived that the principle at stake was vital, involving nothing less than the right of the colonies to govern themselves.

They used to meet in various rooms of the Raleigh Tavern, which is to be seen today in Williamsburg, carefully restored just as it was then. They were resolved to oppose the Townshend Act just as they had opposed the Stamp Act before it.

Sentiment was strong enough, even among the older men, to produce from the Assembly a set of four resolutions opposing the Townshend Act, although probably not as strongly as Jefferson and his friends would have wished. These resolutions were rushed through with the utmost speed so as to get them on the record before the British Governor could have time to act. As soon as they had been voted, and the Governor (now Lord Botetourt) had seen them, he dissolved the Assembly in the name of the King.

Jefferson and his friends, to the number of twenty-eight, took the next step, and it was decisive. There were only twenty-eight of them out of an Assembly of one hundred, but they were determined. When the Assembly was dissolved and closed, and they had nowhere else to go, they met in the Apollo Room of the Raleigh Tavern (just as you will see it today) and decided what to do.

This was the ballroom in which they had all danced and enjoyed themselves for many an evening, and in which many a marriage had been made. It now was the setting for a grimmer job.

The twenty-eight formed what they called the Non-Importation Association and mutually promised to refuse to buy anything from England until the Townshend Act was repealed. They made one exception: paper, which they could not get in the colonies and which was essential to their work.

And moreover, they knew how to enforce their decisions. They went home from Williamsburg and organized committees in every county, in every region, to boycott English goods. It was done with great order but also with great severity. Any merchant who bought or sold English goods was speedily advertised as an enemy of his country and lost all his customers. There were no outrages, no mobs and no destruction. It was done under the direction of leading men in each county, men respected for their honesty and patriotism. Since Virginia was by far the biggest and richest colony in America, and since the boycott was unexpectedly effective, British trade lost the colossal sum of nine hundred thousand pounds (about $4,500,000, but worth at least ten times as much then).

The Townshend Act was repealed. The British parties, both of them, wanted to repeal it all. The Whig Party, led by Chatham and Burke, had always championed the cause of the Americans. The Tories, led by Lord North, realized that the whole taxation act ought to go. North pleaded with his pigheaded King, but George III insisted that at least one tax must be kept, just for the sake of the principle, so as to show that the English Parliament had the right to tax the American colonies without consulting them. And when it came to a vote, it was an exact tie. Poor Lord North, who knew it was wrong, then had to cast the deciding vote himself. The Townshend Act was repealed —all except the tax on tea.

And that, of course, was the real beginning of the American Revolution.

At that time there was very little communication between the colonies, each of which had its separate political organization and was separately governed from London. It took a long time to travel from Massachusetts to Georgia; it was far easier to go to Europe.

The Tea Act of 1773 forced the colonies to turn their eyes toward each other, to get into closer connection, to think of themselves as a related and almost federated association of states. Amongst the first to see this necessity and to try to bring the colonies together was Thomas Jefferson.

You know what happened. Ships laden with tea came over from England and the colonies all refused to let them unload. It was done in different ways in different places. In Philadelphia, for example, the local patriotic committees notified the first ship's captain that any attempt to unload tea would be resisted by force. The captain wisely sailed away, after a while, with his cargo. At Charleston the tea was unloaded but was put into damp caves where it was speedily ruined: not a pound was accepted for sale. In New York a gale drove the tea ship out to sea before it had a chance to attempt an unloading. And in Boston—well, the indignant and organized patriots under Samuel

Adams' direction went out and dumped the ship-load of tea into the harbor.

George III then insisted on punishment. The port of Boston was closed and four regiments of troops ordered there for a military occupation.

Of course Boston was a long way from Virginia and most Virginians had never seen it, but Jefferson and his friends were resolved to make common cause with the Bostonians in this matter which concerned them all. They tried to think of something that would make everybody in Virginia realize that a solemn moment in their history had arrived. Jefferson came up with the idea which was adopted: to proclaim June first (the day the British were to close Boston port) a day of fasting and prayer.

This was June 1, 1774. It was the first time that any such dramatic gesture of unity had been made from one colony to another, and it had to be done in as impressive a manner as possible. Jefferson and his friends thought that the right man to propose it was Robert Carter Nicholas, a member of the Assembly who belonged to the "Old Guard" school, an aristocrat, a man of grave, religious character. He was among those whom Jefferson's friends had pushed aside in their "forward" movement.

Nicholas accepted and proposed the day of fasting and prayer in the Virginia Assembly because of the "great dangers to be derived to British America from the hostile invasion of the city of Boston in our sister colony of Massachusetts."

Next day the British Governor dissolved the Assembly for passing such a resolution, and henceforth the Virginians ran an Assembly of their own.

The day of fasting and prayer was observed throughout Virginia with great solemnity. Jefferson then proposed and formed a Committee of Correspondence (from the outlawed Assembly) which got into communication at once with the committees in all the other colonies with the idea of meeting in "general Congress" to discuss "the united interests of America."

An election was held to a new Virginia Assembly and to choose delegates for the First Continental Congress. Jefferson was inevitably a member of both. The young man's hour of destiny was at hand.

His first great work in the Virginia Convention, as they called this new assembly, was a masterly pamphlet called *A Summary View of the Rights of British America*. Nobody had ever gone so far in asserting the right, "which Nature has given to all men," to move from one country to another and establish new societies under self-given laws. Jefferson saw no more reason why the English in England should make laws for the Americans than that the Saxons of North Europe should make laws for their descendants, the English. Flatly and yet with a genuine mastery of expression, he denied the British Parliament any authority over the American colonies.

The Virginia Convention was not ready for such strong meat, and yet the pamphlet, tabled in the Convention hall to be read by every member, made a very deep impression. It was then printed and circulated throughout the thirteen colonies, where the new ideas took root within a few months and were hotly defended in the North as in the South.

The *Summary View* contained a stern attack on the institution of slavery, which, as Jefferson said, was "unhappily" introduced to the colonies "in their infant state." For this he blamed the British, who refused to allow the colonies to prohibit the importation of slaves from Africa, thus "preferring the advantages of a few British corsairs to the lasting interest of the American States, and to the rights of human nature, deeply wounded by this infamous practice."

Furthermore, he attacked the land system and the right of the King to grant lands in the new world.

He ended with a direct appeal to George III to settle with the colonies on just terms. His final words were: "The God who gave us life, gave us liberty at the same time; the hand of force can destroy, but cannot disjoin them."

The paper not only traveled all over America in a short time, but was also reprinted in London and made its effect there. Edmund Burke, the brilliant Whig orator who had consistently supported the American cause, was responsible for its printing and distribution in England. From this

time on, Jefferson was no longer simply a Virginian, but a national figure—an American.

It was the next year (with things going from bad
to worse) when the Richmond Convention, held
in the little wooden church of St. John which still
stands, debated whether to raise a militia for the
defense of the colony. This had already been done
elsewhere (Massachusetts, for instance). It was
in St. John's Church that Patrick Henry made his
most famous speech, listened to by his admiring
friend Jefferson. It is the one which attacks the
cautious members for their talk of peace. "Peace,
peace!" Henry said, "when there is no peace!" He
asked: "Is life so dear or peace so sweet as to be
purchased at the price of chains and slavery?"
And that ending: "I know not what course others
may take, but as for me, give me liberty or give
me death."

And George Washington, too, was with them
now: he had joined Jefferson and Patrick Henry
and Richard Henry Lee in thinking that Virginia
must be ready to fight.

Meanwhile in London fiery debates were taking
place, with the great Lord Chatham, then ill and

old but still the most imposing man in the Parliament, thundering out in defense of the Americans. So much of what was best in England was on the American side in the argument that the King's government felt obliged to make some attempt at reconciliation. They then produced what was called "Lord North's proposals," which in effect would allow the colonies to tax themselves if the home government could name the amount of taxation required.

To this Jefferson was asked to reply in the name of all the colonies. His "Reply to Lord North" is the logical prelude to the Declaration of Independence. He reviewed the "rapid and bold succession of injuries which, during the course of eleven years, have been aimed at these colonies," and quoted some of the violent statements made against America by men of the government. In the last sentence of this great letter he asks if the world can be "deceived into an opinion that we are unreasonable, or hesitate to believe with us that nothing but our own exertions may defeat the ministerial sentence of death or submission."

Then came the Continental Congress, the First (1774) and the Second (1775), both in Philadelphia, then the largest city in the colonies. The rich of Philadelphia were conservatives, merchants for the most part, and their influence was to hold back on any extreme statement of patriotism. There were Tories of influence in both Congresses, particularly from New York. But there were also determined men such as Sam Adams of Boston, old and poor and careless of appearances, who knew exactly what had to be done. With Sam Adams and with others of his kind Jefferson and his Virginia friends felt the kinship of a new nation.

It was a long fight, with endless talk and many raw tempers. In the First Continental Congress nobody dared talk of independence, and few thought of it; in the Second Continental Congress it had become inevitable. There was an army in the field, commanded by George Washington. Every colony had its militia. Blood had been shed already.

For in the year of 1775-1776 George III had gone to the limit of his stubbornness. The Americans must be beaten into "absolute submission," he said. Nothing else would do. And since Englishmen were reluctant to fight their own relations in the colonies, he would get Germans to do it. He scraped up troops from the small states of Germany, many of them ruled by his own relations, and bought them at so much a head to fight in America. He let criminals out of jail on condition that they would fight in the colonies. He used the "press gang" system to kidnap men from the slums of the great English cities. And meanwhile in his own Parliament some of the greatest voices of the day were incessantly raised in defense of the Americans. By this time it was not only Whigs and oppositionists, but many Tories as well, who saw that George III was about to lose a very great empire.

With things in this state it was natural that Jefferson, already the author of the two principal statements made for the American colonies, should come to the fore in Congress and should take a leading part in the decisions made. He was for independence. When, after the terrible confusion of a debate which seemed to have no end, the Congress decided for independence, Jefferson was asked to write the resolution.

This was in June, 1776, a desperately hot month in Philadelphia, and the delegates (especially Jefferson) seem to have suffered greatly from a plague

They debated every word of the Declaration of Independence.

of horseflies. Jefferson was one of a committee of five, with John Adams and others, but he alone was entrusted with the actual writing of the Declaration of Independence. He toiled over the first draft for two full days, and submitted it to Adams and Franklin before he found the right form to submit to Congress. It went to Congress on June 28, was debated on July 2, 3 and 4, and was finally adopted as the Declaration of Independence on July 4, 1776.

How new and strange all this was we can hardly imagine today. The thirteen colonies had been, up to now, like thirteen different countries. With bad roads, poor communications in general, no great cities and no great newspapers, the links between them had always been very few. It was, as we have said before, simpler to go to London than to a distant sister-colony.

Now the colonial delegates in Congress assembled were asked to declare themselves a nation, a people, independent by natural right, even though they had no combined system of government— no constitution, no head, no method of proceeding as a nation.

It is not surprising that many men balked at the

Declaration of Independence. Many thought it was madness, that the colonies would be overwhelmed by British troops and severely punished, that the uneasy combination of thirteen quite different states would never stand up under the strain of war. Delegates from New York and Pennsylvania, in particular, were shocked at the "radical" nature of the Declaration, and a good many of them went home rather than sign it or vote for it.

But Thomas Jefferson believed in every word of it and had written it in the white heat of a great patriotic passion.

For any other man this might have been the climax of a life or at least of a public career. For Jefferson it was little more than a beginning. He had begun before, of course, but this was his highest statement and remains his masterpiece. Yet from that masterpiece of 1776 to his death, fifty long years afterwards, he was incessantly busy and performed some of the greatest services ever given by one man to his own country.

What were those services?

As a member of Congress and of the Virginia Legislature, as Governor of Virginia, as diplomat abroad, as President and as a citizen in retirement, he fought all his life long for "human rights." Much of what we take for granted today was provided for us by him. He did not always win his fights. Notably, he made no great change in the institution of slavery, although he declared plainly that "if these people are not set free, worse will come." He could not bring about the great system of public education which he tried to create: he was too far ahead of his time. But he did bring into being, for the first time in the Christian world, a law providing for religious freedom, a whole set of constitutional amendments providing for civil rights, innumerable social and economic improvements (such as equal inheritance for all children, male or female) and a general climate of democratic freedom, or aspiration toward democratic freedom, which is today the American air.

And perhaps because it is as natural as the air we breathe, we take it all for granted.

The young man who toiled in the heat of Philadelphia, tortured by the flies as he wrote, was by this time well aware of what he was doing. The language of the Declaration of Independence is on a very high level of historic consciousness—

that is, it shows that its author was fully conscious of the meaning and consequences of the words. Jefferson knew that a long and exhausting war must follow this: it lasted seven years. He knew that his appeal must be to the world in general, because only by the world's help—or some help from the rest of the world—could the colonies win against England's might. This help, as we know, did come, chiefly from France.

He knew that you cannot declare your independence for such lofty reasons of "natural right" and "natural equality" without carrying through: that is, if the colonies won their independence, they would have to try very hard to make men equal and free. This meant that a lot of the old laws and privileges and class rule must be destroyed. Otherwise the Declaration of Independence would have been so much prattle: and to Jefferson it was no prattle.

In fact he framed the Declaration of Independence in such a way that it can be seen to have determined an enormous amount of the subsequent history of the United States.

For nearly two hundred years all Americans have studied this short document and a great many have memorized it in whole or in part. It is a part of the American mind.

Therefore expressions like "Life, Liberty and the pursuit of Happiness," as being "inalienable Rights," have entered into everything we think. That governments "derive their just powers from the consent of the governed," and that it is a right and a duty to overthrow any government which becomes absolute despotism—that it is wrong to "render the military independent of and superior to the civil power"—all these and many more ideas in the Declaration have woven themselves into the entire habit of American thought. Following out such ideas most of our development has taken place, and if you read sufficiently between the lines you can in fact see almost our entire history foreshadowed in this Declaration of Independence, as it was written by Jefferson at the age of thirty-three.

An inspiration of more than common force must have pushed his pen. It came, of course, from his whole preceding life, all his studies, all his work and dreams. He had lived his thirty-three years for this hour. He had studied law, government and politics, had absorbed particularly the ideas of

Greece and Rome, had been influenced by English philosophy of the liberal kind. But it is true also that his natural attachment to ideas of freedom, which he seems to have had from his earliest years (perhaps because of the spectacle of slavery before him), was the spark that set all this off into the shower of brilliance which is the Declaration.

The ideas themselves were not Jefferson's alone. Many men in the Continental Congress thought the same way. There was no one else who could have put it all down with such power and precision.

And there were many who disliked this or that or the other idea in the Declaration. They voted for it just the same because on the whole, taken all together, it was the loftiest presentation of the colonies' case that could be made, and was most likely to appeal to the outside world.

One part which had been written with all of Jefferson's heart, mind and soul was cut out. That was a denunciation of slavery as having been forced on the colonies by the British slave traders. Many in the South objected, and it gave offense to the delegates from Massachusetts, whose own people had been slave traders just as much as the British. The paragraph was sacrificed. It cost Massachusetts—as well as Virginia—a great deal to get rid of slavery; it cost the American people a terrible civil war; but Jefferson was too far ahead of his time. Nobody would pay attention to his ideas on the subject then.

They were anxious days for him. For just at this time, when he wrote the great Declaration and saw it through the days of debate, his wife Martha was seriously ill. He was waiting for couriers from Monticello all the time, every day. He went to Monticello when he could, in the intervals of the Congress, but it was a long, hard journey from Philadelphia. In his anxiety for wife and family, for his beloved house as well (which was then in a spurt of building), he may sometimes have wondered, as he did often afterwards, why public life had so taken possession of him.

For one of the odd things about Jefferson was that although he was a public man almost from birth, interested above all things in public affairs, born to debate and to rule, he never ceased to long for private life, his family and his farm.

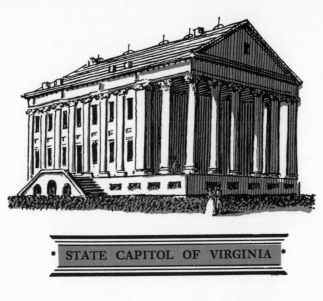

4 · The Battle Won

MARTHA WAS NEVER WELL AGAIN AFTER 1776, and she died six years later. Jefferson, although relatively a young man, never remarried. The gracious shade of Martha Jefferson, as we can see it today when we look at her harpsichord at Monticello, was his lifelong companion. He later came under the influence of a number of beautiful and intelligent women, particularly in Paris, but since their part in his life was small they do not concern this story.

His main job, as he regarded it, was to set things

IN CONGRESS.

The unanimous Declaration of the thirteen united...

When in the Course of human events, it becomes necessary for one people to d...
of some among the powers of the earth, the separate and equal station to which the Laws of Nature and of Nature's God en...
should declare the causes which impel them to the separation. _____ We hold these truths to be self-evi...
with certain unalienable Rights, that among these are Life, Liberty and the pursuit of Happiness. — That to sec...
powers from the consent of the governed, — That whenever any Form of Government becomes destructive of these ends...
Government, laying its foundation on such principles and organizing its powers in such form, as to them shall se...
will dictate that Governments long established should not be changed for light and transient causes; and accordingly...
evils are sufferable, than to right themselves by abolishing the forms to which they are accustomed. But when a long...
evinces a design to reduce them under absolute Despotism, it is their right, it is their duty, to throw off such Governm...
been the patient sufferance of these Colonies; and such is now the necessity which constrains them to alter their former...
Britain is a history of repeated injuries and usurpations, all having in direct object the establishment of an absolute T...
world. _____ He has refused his Assent to Laws, the most wholesome and necessary for the public good...
and pressing importance, unless suspended in their operation till his Assent should be obtained; and when so suspen...
pass other Laws for the accommodation of large districts of people, unless those people would relinquish the right of Repre...
to tyrants only. _____ He has called together legislative bodies at places unusual, uncomfortable, and distant from the...
compliance with his measures. _____ He has dissolved Representative Houses repeatedly, for opposing with manly...
along time, after such dissolutions, to cause others to be elected; whereby the Legislative powers, incapable of Annihilat...
ing in the mean time exposed to all the dangers of invasion from without, and convulsions within. _____ He has en...
ting the Laws for Naturalization of Foreigners; refusing to pass others to encourage their migrations hither, and raising the...
Administration of Justice, by refusing his Assent to Laws for establishing judiciary powers. _____ He has made...
and payment of their salaries. _____ He has erected a multitude of New Offices, and sent hither swarms of Officers...
us, in times of peace, Standing Armies without the Consent of our legislatures. _____ He has affected to render the Militar...
with others to subject us to a jurisdiction foreign to our constitution, and unacknowledged by our laws; giving his As...
armed troops among us: — For protecting them, by a mock Trial, from punishment for any Murders which they...
our Trade with all parts of the world: — For imposing Taxes on us without our Consent: — For depriving us in...
has to be tried for pretended offences — For abolishing the free System of English Laws in a neighbouring Provin...
as to render it at once an example and fit instrument for introducing the same absolute rule into these Colonies: ...
altering fundamentally the Forms of our Governments: — For suspending our own Legislatures, and declaring the...
He has abdicated Government here, by declaring us out of his Protection and waging War against us. _____ He ha...
of our people. _____ He is at this time transporting large Armies of foreign Mercenaries to compleat the works of death,...
scarcely paralleled in the most barbarous ages, and totally unworthy the Head of a civilized nation. _____ He has constr...
their country, to become the executioners of their friends and Brethren, or to fall themselves by their Hands. _____ He has e...
inhabitants of our frontiers, the merciless Indian Savages, whose known rule of warfare, is an undistinguished destruction of...
have Petitioned for Redress in the most humble terms: Our repeated Petitions have been answered by repeated injury. A...
is unfit to be the ruler of a free people. _____ Nor have We been wanting in attentions to our British brethren. We have wa...
able jurisdiction over us. We have reminded them of the circumstances of our emigration and settlement here: We have a...
by the ties of our common kindred to disavow these usurpations, which, would inevitably interrupt our connections and...
consanguinity. We must, therefore, acquiesce in the necessity, which denounces our Separation, and hold them, as we...

We, therefore, the Representatives of the united States of America, in General Congress, A...
tention, do, in the Name, and by Authority of the good People of these Colonies, solemnly publish and declare, That...
States; that they are Absolved from all Allegiance to the British Crown, and that all political connection between...
that as Free and Independent States; they have full Power to levy War, conclude Peace, contract Alliances, establish...
States may of right do. _____ And for the support of this Declaration, with a firm reliance on the Protection of...
and our sacred Honor. _____

John Hancock

Button Gwinnett
Lyman Hall
Geo Walton.

Wm Hooper
Joseph Hewes.
John Penn

Edward Rutledge.

Thos Heyward Junr.
Thomas Lynch Junr.
Arthur Middleton

Samuel Chase
Wm Paca
Thos Stone
Charles Carroll of Carrollton

George Wythe
Richard Henry Lee
Th Jefferson
Benja Harrison
Thos Nelson jr.
Francis Lightfoot Lee
Carter Braxton

JULY 4, 1776.

States of America.

WHEN in the Course of human events, it becomes necessary for one people to dissolve the political bands which have connected them with another, and to assume among the Powers of the earth, the separate and equal station to which the Laws of Nature and of Nature's God entitle them, a decent respect to the opinions of mankind requires that they should declare the causes which impel them to the separation.

We hold these truths to be self-evident, that all men are created equal, that they are endowed by their Creator with certain unalienable Rights, that among these are Life, Liberty and the Pursuit of Happiness. That to secure these rights, Governments are instituted among Men, deriving their just powers from the consent of the governed, That whenever any Form of Government becomes destructive of these ends, it is the Right of the People to alter or to abolish it, and to institute new Government, laying its foundation on such principles and organizing its powers in such form, as to them shall seem most likely to effect their Safety and Happiness.

* * *

And for the support of this Declaration, with a firm reliance on the Protection of Divine Providence, we mutually pledge to each other our Lives, our Fortunes, and our sacred Honor.

from the Declaration of Independence

straight in his own native place, the state of Virginia. He had written the Declaration of Independence on the highest possible plane of aspiration. He knew it was a historic document. Now he had to make it come true.

For words, words alone, as Jefferson knew better than most people because he possessed them and could command them, were not enough. If you declared your independence for the sake of human rights then you must do your level best to ensure that the people all around you actually had these human rights.

In October, 1776, three months after the Declaration of Independence, Jefferson went back to the Legislature of Virginia in order to see that the laws of his own beloved state would conform, as closely as he could make them conform, to the high ideals he had proclaimed for the whole country.

There were many injustices to set right. Slavery, as we have already remarked, was too much for him. It was the system of the country and by this time was too deeply embedded in all the social and economic machinery to be changed by Jefferson's unaided words. But there were many things he could do. He was one of the ablest lawyers in the country, its finest writer of public or state papers, its most inflexible conscience and one of its best brains. Many and many a time what he had to propose was far in advance of the thinking current amongst those around him. They rejected his ideas, or were very reluctant to accept them. And yet they could not turn them down offhand, without reflection, because by now they all knew that this Tom Jefferson was a very remarkable man and might be—as he had proved—right. Thus to his inherited advantages of family and fortune, which had guaranteed him a hearing to start with, Jefferson now had added the prestige of talent. He always used to say that he believed in only one kind of aristocracy, "the aristocracy of virtue and talent."

His great efforts in the Virginia legislature were for religious freedom, a reform of the inheritance system on estates, and public education. He succeeded in most of this, but not, unfortunately, in education. What he proposed in that respect is more or less what we have today, but it was too early for the landowning aristocrats of Virginia to accept the notion that the state ought to provide education for everybody.

The other Jeffersonian reforms went through. He had always disliked "entail" (the system by which an estate would pass intact from generation to generation, could not be broken up or sold). He thought it was one of the main props of feudalism, a barrier to any real democracy. He also opposed "primogeniture," by which the eldest son always inherited the estate no matter how many younger sons or daughters there might be. These two things, by which he had himself benefited of course, were the target of his attack for years. He got entail abolished in 1776, his first year in the free legislature, but primogeniture did not go until nine years later when he was living in Paris as American Minister. The law he had written was put through by his new and devoted follower, the young lawyer James Monroe. Indeed, although Jefferson's work was all his own, much of it could never have been enacted into law if he had not possessed such valiant friends as Monroe and Madi-

son, who carried on when his duties took him elsewhere.

What Jefferson valued above all in his work for
Virginia was the enactment of a law providing for
religious freedom.

It is hard nowadays to imagine what the situation was then with respect to religious beliefs and
church memberships. Everybody had to pay for
the upkeep of the established state church—that
is, the Church of England, which was to become the Episcopal Church of the United States.
Virginia was in the diocese of the Bishop of
London and conformed to the English customs and
laws. However, during the preceding hundred
years a great many people had grown tired of the
established church, with its fox-hunting parsons
and generally lax and worldly manners. Baptists,
Methodists and Quakers converted many Virginians to their forms of belief. Religious reviv-
als and waves of religious feeling tended to
be within these new forms rather than inside the
old church.

But under the law nobody had a right to be a

Baptist, Methodist or Quaker. The laws were not always strictly applied, but in fact it was possible, and quite often happened, that a man could be thrown into jail for preaching what he believed.

The turmoil that followed when Jefferson drew up the Statute of Virginia for Religious Freedom seems hard to understand today. We take these freedoms as easily and naturally as we take the climate itself. But there had never been, anywhere in the Christian world, a law declaring that it was the citizen's right to believe and worship as he pleased. The thing was absolutely new. Religious toleration had been practiced in many places and at various times, usually by the simple method of looking the other way when people wished to worship God in a manner different from the majority. The colony of Maryland, founded by Roman Catholics, had always tolerated other beliefs. But Virginia was the first to put it all down in black on white and make a law which proclaimed it as a natural right, never to be broken by the state, for each individual to believe and worship according to his own conscience. Jefferson was so proud of this law that he put it, along with the Declaration of

Independence and the founding of the University of Virginia, on his tombstone: these were the three things he valued highest in his life.

But it took a long time to get the Statute of Religious Freedom enacted. Ten years, in fact. Jefferson had long since gone on to other activities. Again it was his faithful friends who continued to work on his cherished plans—Monroe above all.

Jefferson was fortunate in many things, but one of the luckiest happenings of his life was that fate sent him, at the right time, two devoted disciples who remained faithful to him until death. These were James Madison and James Monroe, who were later on to succeed him in the presidency.

In 1776 Jefferson was thirty-three, Madison was twenty-five and Monroe was only eighteen. Madison went to the Virginia Convention, where he met Jefferson and fell under his spell—"enlisted for life," as has been said. Young Monroe, a promising student at William and Mary, left college just at that time to join the Third Virginia Regiment as a lieutenant and was sent north to serve under Washington in the battles across New Jersey and

Pennsylvania. Four years later (1780) he was released from the army because of wounds and came
to Jefferson, at the age of twenty-two, to study
law. Monroe, also, "enlisted for life."

Madison was a pale and studious young man,
not long down from his studies at Princeton, when
he first met Jefferson. He always was frail and
subject to illnesses but in spite of this fact he had
a tremendous appetite for work, particularly in
Jefferson's service. In the battle for the law on
religious freedom he was Jefferson's lieutenant,
in spite of his youth, and it was the two Jameses,
Madison and Monroe, who continued to fight on
for this cause after their great leader was no longer
in Virginia.

Wherever he went, Jefferson never lost touch
with his two disciples, to whom he wrote a very
large number of letters which have been preserved.
These two were in a way substitutes for the sons
he never had. In one letter years later he tells
Monroe that "you and Mr. Madison are the two
pillars of my happiness." At that time he was well
over sixty years old and was getting ready to retire from the presidency, but his two "pillars of

happiness" had served him well for thirty years.

Madison was the battler for religious freedom at first, and when he went on to the Congress in Philadelphia Monroe became the champion. Meanwhile Jefferson (1779) was "kicked upstairs" and could no longer take any direct part in the struggle: he was removed from the legislature by being made Governor of Virginia. From then on all the legislative battles always had to be fought by others, but Jefferson's advice and directing hand were always there, even though unseen, and from whatever distance.

As Governor of Virginia he had, of course, to take the responsibility for the military safety of the Old Dominion, and this at a time when Washington's army was being hard pushed from all sides, north and south. Washington himself was a Virginian, the most revered of all Virginians, and when he asked for Virginia troops Jefferson never hesitated to send them. For some time this was safe enough: Virginia was not attacked. So the best of Virginia's troops, arms, munitions and money went to defend New York, New Jersey and Pennsylvania.

This was all very well until Virginia herself was attacked and invaded (1780-81), when there was hardly anything at Jefferson's disposal to oppose to the British army. Only the young Marquis de Lafayette with a handful of troops came down from the north, but he had not enough men to do more than skirmish skilfully and retreat. Richmond was burned; Jefferson himself and his whole government narrowly escaped being captured by a daring raid of British cavalry which dashed in as far as Monticello.

Young Colonel James Monroe, who was not yet sure whether he was studying law or continuing as a soldier, was of great use to Jefferson in those trying days. It was just then that he wrote to Jefferson—he was barely twenty-two—the heartfelt words: "Had I not formed a connection with you I should most certainly have retired from society. . . . You became acquainted with me and undertook the direction of my studies and believed in me. I feel that whatever I am at present in the opinion of others, or whatever I may be in the future, has greatly arisen from your friendship."

The war of the Revolution ended, as everybody

The British surrendered to Washington at Yorktown.

knows, in Virginia. Washington at last heeded Jefferson's desperate appeals and came on south with the main body of his army; General Greene came up from the Carolinas, and the French regulars under Count Rochambeau, newly landed, put themselves under Washington's command. Lord Cornwallis, the British commander, had been amusing himself by chasing "the boy"—young Lafayette —all around Virginia, hoping to catch him as a prize exhibit for London. Lafayette, in spite of his youth, was too skilful and hardy to be caught. Cornwallis then fortified himself in the village of Yorktown, down at the end of the peninsula, and Washington besieged him there. The French fleet, under DeGrasse, came up just in time to cut off the escape by sea, and defeated a British fleet which came up to relieve the situation. Cornwallis, after several weeks of this siege on all sides, had to surrender his entire army. It was the end of the war.

Colonel James Monroe was then barely 23; Lafayette was the same age; George Washington's other aide, Alexander Hamilton, was 24. Jefferson at 38 seemed an elder statesman to all of them,

but even he bowed, as did everybody in the thirteen states at this solemn moment of victory, to
General George Washington, the oldest of them
all. Washington himself was not an old man—he
was 49—but he had towered over all of them for
years and they felt, as the whole country did, that
the victory was his.

Jefferson's term as Governor of Virginia came
to an end just before the climax of the war; he was
succeeded by Thomas Nelson, and then had a little
time of his own at Monticello. These intervals—
whenever he could get them—were precious to
him, for he never stopped building his house,
gardens, stables, outhouses, greenhouses, parks and
roads. He was in no mood for public office. Many
people thought this was because the Virginia legislature had been critical of him for sending troops
to Washington when the Old Dominion itself was
in danger. The truth was that Martha Jefferson, his
beloved wife, was dying, and did indeed die in September, 1782. Jefferson could not leave her. He
refused an appointment which the Congress wished
to give him for France, and refused likewise to
accept a candidacy—a sure-fire candidacy—for the

Congress itself. Madison and Monroe, as well as many other faithful followers, were discouraged at this retirement because they all thought the country needed Jefferson; Monroe, the most candid of them, wrote to say so.

But even as he watched in grief over his dying wife, Jefferson was busy. It was in his nature to keep occupied, whatever happened. A Frenchman named Marbois, attached to the French mission in Philadelphia, submitted to him a long list of questions about Virginia, asking for answers to them and any related information. Jefferson spent many weeks during the year 1781 writing out this information, which was to appear some years later as a book under the name of *Notes on Virginia*. It is the only more or less professional book he ever wrote—at all events, the only one he ever published himself. On natural history, on the Indians, on geography and a thousand other subjects, it was the most complete account yet given of the immense territory still comprised in the state of Virginia.

After Martha's death he had no reason for refusing public duty, and accepted the appointment to join Benjamin Franklin, John Adams and John Jay overseas in negotiating a peace treaty with England. Before he could arrange his journey to Europe the peace treaty was signed, and he turned homewards again, only to be chosen—before he even got there—as representative in the Congress.

Jefferson was only in the Congress for two years, but his service there was remarkable in its results. For one thing, he became responsible for the dollar as it exists today—that is, a decimal coinage easily understood by everybody, based on the Spanish dollar. This was achieved by a report on money, originally by Robert Morris, which was logical but a little too logical. It called for a unit which would be the 140th part of a Spanish dollar and then built up from that base in tens. Jefferson, reviewing this report, accepted the decimal idea, but simplified it by just dividing the Spanish dollar into a hundred parts and calling the penny the unit. Thus he created the money which has endured ever since.

He saw the peace treaty through Congress, also, and then turned to his greatest work. As we know, Virginia's territory was a vast empire taking in what are now among the richest states of the Union, the so-called Northwest Territory, Illinois and Michigan and the rest. Jefferson had long wanted Virginia to give this great empire to the Federal Union. When at last, in 1784, it was possible to do so, a strange and rather disgusting drama took place: the Federal Union was not allowed to accept the gift for a long time because of the influence of a band of land speculators and land companies. These people, who had illegally purchased land from Indians for next to nothing, now claimed that the land had been in the public domain from the beginning. There was an unpleasant odor of corruption over the whole thing, as a good many congressmen were involved in the shady transactions, but in the end decency and common sense triumphed and the Western Territories of Virginia were accepted by the nation.

Jefferson was named head of the committee to draw up a scheme of government for the Northwest Territory. In his scheme the most important thing was a clause saying that slavery would not be permitted there, in the whole area west of a line beginning at Lake Erie drawn south, after the year 1800. In this Jefferson was laying down for the first time the principle that slavery should be hemmed in so that eventually it would die of itself. His idea was to stop the slave trade as soon as possible, restrict slavery to the old slave states, make all the new westward territories free, and thus bring about a state of things in which slavery would pass away naturally without a struggle.

Curiously enough, although Jefferson was again ahead of his time and could not bring all this to pass, the idea never perished. Sixty-five years later Abraham Lincoln went into the presidency holding exactly the same idea and the same program, to restrict slavery to the old slave states and let it die there.

Jefferson's anti-slavery clause was stricken out of the Ordinance for the Northwest Territory in 1784, but three years later (after he had gone to France), it was put back in again for the northern part. The states of the great triangle between the Mississippi and the Ohio rivers became free territory in 1800 and remained free ever afterwards. The southern area (Alabama, Mississippi) was slave land. Practically speaking, this may have been one of Jefferson's greatest contributions to the making of America, as it probably saved the Union in the Civil War and made Abe Lincoln's work possible.

But by the time the question was settled Jefferson was in Paris. In 1784 he was named an assistant to Benjamin Franklin and John Adams in making commercial treaties with European nations; then, a year later, he became minister to France, succeeding old Franklin.

His years in Paris were happy and interesting to him. He had the liveliest curiosity for everybody and everything. Scientists, fine ladies, street waifs and courtiers might come under his observation in a single morning. He was well received everywhere, for his gifts of charm and learning were considerable, and he spoke excellent French. Besides, the Americans were rather fashionable just then, even in the highest court circles of the absolute monarchy, because the American Revolution—succeeding with French assistance—had been something new and strange in human history. Franklin, old Franklin, had been the darling of the most refined and exalted circles. Jefferson was not

THE DIE-HARDS

quite such a character as Franklin. ("No, I do not replace Dr. Franklin," he had said to the French minister of foreign affairs. "I succeed him. Nobody could replace him.") But he had his own commanding intellect, his wide range of scientific and philosophical interest, and his handsome house was open to all. In fact he kept open house in Paris—just as he did everywhere else—to such an extent that his own private purse suffered a great deal: the Congress never would pay the expenses of the life he was obliged to lead.

The French Revolution was brewing, was about to come to a head. Those were exciting days in Paris to anybody with a sense of history, and Jefferson had about as good a sense of history, past, present and future, as existed in his time.

Lafayette used to come to see him constantly, and brought along a number of the other younger men who wanted to reform the French monarchy without sweeping it away. These men were not the rabid revolutionaries and terrorists of later days, whose way of dealing with the aristocrats was to chop off their heads; indeed many of these men (including Lafayette, of course) were themselves aristocrats of the oldest families. They were the "liberals," those who wanted to reform the state, give some self-government to the people, relieve the pressures on finance by taxing the rich, and abolish all the old privileges of aristocracy and clergy. They were Jefferson's friends, thought along his lines and in part did so because of his teaching. His *Notes on Virginia* had been published in Paris, and by this time his Declaration of Independence was a familiar document to all the smart people of Paris, even at the court of Louis XVI and Marie Antoinette.

Jefferson's return to America was, after five years, only supposed to be for a short leave. He wanted to bring his daughter Martha home. She had been taught at a convent in Paris during these years, where her younger sister Mary (called "Polly") joined her after a while. But in time Martha grew to be almost too French. Her father decided she needed her own country again, and asked for leave to go home. He took the long journey, and when he got off the ship he found out by the newspapers that George Washington had named him Secretary of State in the first American government to be formed under the new Constitution.

5 · To the White House

JEFFERSON SERVED FOUR YEARS AS SECRE-
tary of State under George Washington and four
years as Vice-President under John Adams. In
both of those offices he was removed in part from
the public battle. He could not go into the Congress
and engage in debate or offer his views, any more
than a Secretary of State or Vice-President can
today. As Secretary he had to run his department
and attend cabinet meetings, putting his views in
ways which were more or less private, and allow-
ing others to make the public speeches. As Vice-

President he was even more restricted, presiding over the Senate—with complete impartiality according even to his enemies—but doing little else.

These were the rules and he kept them.

And yet there was nothing to prevent his keeping up a steady private correspondence with those who, like Madison and Monroe, looked to him for guidance in all matters. His views were strong. He believed in civil rights, or the legal aspect of human rights, above all else, and his correspondence from Paris on the subject was incessant. His main criticism of the new Constitution was that it contained no provisions for civil rights at all. No matter how good a government may be, he contended over and over again, the ordinary citizen must have some protection against it.

A citizen must have the protection of *habeas corpus*—that is, there must be a warrant sworn out upon a specific crime before he can be arrested. Nobody can be held in jail without this warrant upon complaint, or otherwise the writ of *habeas corpus* is invoked and the citizen must be released. This very old protection of English common law was not in our Constitution as adopted in 1787.

A citizen should have the right to speak or write freely, to assemble with other citizens freely, and to petition the government when he wishes to do so.

A citizen ought to be safe from unwarranted invasion of his house, papers and property; he ought to be free from having soldiers quartered upon him in peacetime; he ought to be able to bear arms if he is expected to be in the militia; he should have jury trial and defense by counsel when he is tried for a crime.

No citizen ought to be put twice in danger of his life or limb for suspicion of the same offense, nor should he be compelled to be a witness against himself in any criminal case; nor should he be deprived of life, liberty or property without "due process of law."

Even in common law, wherever the values disputed amount to more than $20, the citizen has the right to trial by jury.

There ought never to be strange, cruel punishments ("cruel and unusual") inflicted by the courts, and no citizen should be held to excessive bail.

All these and similar ideas constitute the "civil rights" of the citizen, hard-earned rights which centuries of English common law had preserved. Jefferson valued them almost beyond any political rights that could be named, and he was incessantly troubled during his years in Paris by the fact that the new Constitution was being made without them. Over and over again he wrote to Madison, Monroe, Adams, Jay and others, setting forth his point of view. The Constitution was framed in his absence, just the same, and without any guaranty of civil rights at all.

To this he reacted with characteristic energy, and his influence even at a distance was very great. Even the august Washington, so much above the battle that he took no part in most discussions, was made aware of Jefferson's views. It was, in fact, downright impossible to ignore the views of the man who wrote the Declaration of Independence, which remained (even after the Constitution was adopted) the fundamental document of the American Republic.

Madison and Monroe had no desire to ignore Jefferson, who remained their idol. Madison had played a great part, along with Hamilton and Jay and others, in the making of the Constitution, and had only left out the civil rights clauses in order to get the main political structure accepted first. He had always intended to get the civil rights clauses into the document in time.

Alexander Hamilton, the brilliant spokesman of the rich and privileged classes, cared little about civil rights but had no rooted objection to them. His main concern was to get a firm central government established and keep out of it as many of the people as possible. He wanted either a king or a president elected for life; he wanted strong federal powers, many restrictions on the right to vote, and as clearly as possible, a government by men of property only. Great genius and patriot though he was, he was not a native American and said so a number of times in his letters—the general climate of democracy did not suit him at all. Because of his sincere dislike for democracy, Alexander Hamilton, the lowly and penniless immigrant from the West Indies, became the champion of aristocracy, as against Thomas Jefferson, the Vir-

ginia aristocrat and landowner who spent his life trying to achieve a democratic society.

It was not at all difficult, once the political structure of the United States had been set up in the main body of the Constitution, to get the Bill of Rights added on as a series of amendments. It was not difficult, but nobody knows how much was due to the steady, obstinate insistence of Thomas Jefferson. Behind the scenes, having no part in the matter, he never stopped prodding and poking at his friends and acquaintances. There is no doubt that he enlisted George Washington in the same cause, although Washington would have done no more than drop a word or two now and then.

Anyhow, the first ten amendments to the Constitution were proposed in 1789 (the year before Jefferson became Secretary of State) and took the usual long, slow course toward adoption (passage by both houses of Congress and ratification by three-fourths of the State legislatures). In 1791 they were finally adopted and have remained ever since as the principal safeguard of the American citizen against any abuse of power on the part of his government.

The first American government—that of George Washington—was very different in almost every way from the governments of the next hundred and fifty years or so. Washington kept a sort of stately style like a monarch, and his wife—called "Madam Washington" or even "Lady Washington" in the newspapers—received as if she were a queen. They and the Congress used New York as a capital to begin with and afterwards Philadelphia. In both cases a kind of court society circulated around them. Washington, who was already beginning his decline and was extremely easily bored, took little part either in politics or in ordinary conversation. His prestige in the country was enormous. He was in fact the only man who was ever unanimously elected to the presidency—every elector voted for him. One slight word from him counted more than a whole speech or series of speeches from somebody else. But most of the time he did not bother.

We have descriptions of the dinners given by George and Martha Washington which give a

measure of the extreme boredom felt by everybody. Washington practically never spoke. He
used to play with his fork against the table from
time to time while others spoke. At the end of
the meal there were solemn toasts all round, in
wine—each guest was toasted—and then the ladies
rose and left the room. After that, in a very few
minutes the dinner was over.

At cabinet meetings, also, Washington was
usually silent. He did pay attention to what was
said, and many times over he was able to retain
decorum and some kind of friendly feeling by his
own native dignity, as well as by the respect they
all owed him.

But friendly feeling was hard to maintain. For
the fact was that the cabinet was divided. There
were no political parties as yet. There had come
into being a kind of loose name-calling device by
which those who held, with Hamilton, for a strong
central government, were called Federalists, and
those who opposed this strong central government
were anti-Federalists.

However, this was a deceptive pair of labels.
Jefferson himself said he was not a Federalist be-

cause he objected to the absence of a civil rights
declaration in the Constitution and because he
objected to the provision that a president could
be re-elected indefinitely, for any number of terms.
But he also said that he was much further from
being an anti-Federalist. The anti-Federalists were
those who, believing in states' rights and sover-
eignty to an extreme degree, would have had only
a weak confederation of states with a nominal
central authority in foreign affairs and the like
but no real contact with or direct power over the
individual citizen.

In another way of putting it, the Federalists
wished to govern not only the states but the citizens of the states. The anti-Federalists thought
the central government should deal only with the
state governments and have nothing to do with
their citizens.

One side would have made a nation out of the
thirteen separate parts. The other side said there
were in fact thirteen separate nations in a confed-
eracy of convenience for certain matters such as
relations with Europe, etc.

One way of forcing a nation into existence, as

the genius of Alexander Hamilton saw, was to tax the whole people from and for the federal government, and to make the whole people responsible for all the debts that had been piled up during the Revolution by the separate states. These most decisive weapons, reaching at the people through their pocketbooks, would do more to make the country one and indivisible than all the laws that could have been invented and passed.

So Hamilton proceeded to do so.

He "funded" all the debts of the Revolution, whether they were of the Continental Congress or of the individual states; he guaranteed all the "scrip" of the war days at par. Washington, who had made him Secretary of the Treasury, supported him in these acts, although there was a tremendous outburst of speculation around them. Many ordinary soldiers of the Revolution had sold their scrip—their bonds—for what they could get, a mere fraction of the face value. Now all this paper was to be redeemed by the Federal Government at its face value.

What is more, the plan leaked out in advance, perhaps because Hamilton himself talked too much of his plans, and the bankers and stockbrokers of New York and Philadelphia had time to buy up an enormous quantity of the old scrip for a song. Great fortunes were made. Even members of Congress participated in the wholesale swindling of poor people who did not know—could not know— the value of the paper they held.

Jefferson hated speculation all his life long. This alone would have been enough to turn him against Hamilton politically. Hamilton made no money at all out of his Treasury operations; he was above suspicion in such ways; but all his friends and relatives profited exceedingly.

Yet quite aside from the Treasury operations, which, with all the bad things that went along with them, did help to make a nation out of the thirteen states, there were plenty of other reasons why Jefferson and Hamilton should come to be opponents. They respected each other, but they disagreed on almost every important point about the nature of government.

Hamilton, twelve years Jefferson's junior, was impetuous, talkative, and tended to a kind of arrogance and impatience which did not allow others much time to present their views. He was strongly in favor of an aristocratic form of government. He would have preferred a monarchy and a hereditary aristocracy if they had been obtainable. Since they were not, he accepted the Constitution as it was framed and fought hard for it, harder than anybody else in the thirteen states, because he thought it was the best that could be had. But he never believed in democracy at all, from beginning to end. His whole effort was to exclude the "rabble"—that is, the people—from government as much as possible, and to concentrate it into the hands of as few as possible, those few being men of property.

Jefferson's whole political existence depended upon his faith in democracy and his lifelong effort to make it wider, stronger and truer. He wanted more voters, not fewer voters. He opposed any kind of aristocratic pretense, privilege, title or assumption. He thought the Presidents should serve one or at most two terms and should be merely citizens like any other, except for the kind of work they did.

It was natural, it could never have been avoided: Jefferson and Hamilton became the symbols of the two opposing tendencies in the new nation. Since they were members of the same cabinet, one at the State Department and the other at the Treasury, their opposition gave rise to some strange circumstances. There was a time when they used to meet in the cabinet, under the grave and even solemn chairmanship of Washington, without even speaking to each other. Washington, who valued them both, had to keep the balance.

And as the French Revolution developed into its later excesses, the Jefferson-Hamilton struggle took a new form. Jefferson was supposed to be a "Jacobin"—that is, in sympathy with the extreme terrorists, those who were cutting off heads in France. This was not true, but since he had sympathized with the earlier and more moderate revolutionists, and since he still regarded the French Revolution (with all its excesses) as a great and necessary historical movement towards progress, he had to swallow a great deal of abuse from the opposite camp.

For the Hamiltonians, which meant nearly all the people of wealth and influence, were against the French Revolution from the beginning. They shed tears and went into mourning when the

French King and his Queen, Marie Antoinette, were beheaded. People in the high society of New York and Philadelphia went so far that no "Democrat," as they were beginning to be called (the followers of Jefferson), would be invited to dinner or to the large parties which were a part of every congressional session. Jefferson, the Secretary of State, and still more a little later Jefferson, the Vice-President, found himself more or less ostracized, and could spend his leisure as he really preferred to do, in studies of philosophy and natural history.

He had, as a matter of fact, a very rough time during part of those twelve years. The press of the cities was largely controlled by the Federalists (Hamiltonians), and at that time there was practically no limit to the abuse they could hand out, personal or political, on Jefferson or his friends. It is notable that he never personally answered attacks upon him, never showed signs of anger, and never at any time believed in curbs upon the freedom of the press to say whatever it pleased.

The mass of the people was in favor of Jefferson and in favor also of the French Revolution. When the new French Republic sent an envoy to

America—the foolish and indiscreet Citizen Genêt
—great crowds of admirers cheered him in the
streets. But the Hamiltonians, who had the money,
the influence and the power through Washington's
two administrations and that of John Adams afterwards, saw to it that the weight of the American
government inclined more and more toward the
English side in the struggle between France and
England.

Jefferson, tired of the fruitless debate, resigned
as Secretary of State in 1793. He had tried to do
so several times before, but Washington persuaded
him to stay on, even though Hamilton and Hamilton's ideas were in full control of the government.
For three years Jefferson was permitted again to
live at Monticello, his beloved hilltop, and take
care of his family, his house and his crops.

But he was not really in retirement—he could
never really be in retirement again. His party was
actually created during these years and the four
that followed. There was a steady procession of
politicians and patriots to his door. He was at all
times the idol of the American people. His great
struggle in Virginia itself for civil rights, religious
freedom and democracy in all matters, including

education, had been understood from one end of the country to the other. Most of all, his Declaration of Independence had already become a statement growing Americans memorized and fed their minds upon. He was the people's chosen leader, as he remained until his death.

Hamilton, on the other hand, his great and temporarily successful rival, meant nothing to the bulk of the people. To tell the truth, Hamilton's contempt for the ordinary people was so open, so clearly expressed, that it seems he never really attached any value to popularity. He never tried to be elected to any office: he held the Treasury (until 1795 when he retired) and that was all. In the Treasury and from the Treasury he controlled the entire government, including at some crucial times the State Department as well. His influence upon Washington was undoubtedly great. He had gone to Washington as a young volunteer, had been an aide-de-camp to the great commander throughout the Revolution, and had written most of the letters and state papers to which George Washington's name was signed. When Washington decided to retire from public life and made his great Farewell Address to the

JEFFERSON versus HAMILTON

American people, it was Hamilton, according to the weight of evidence, who wrote the words.

Hamilton left the Treasury (1795) in order to retire to private law practice in New York and make some money for himself and his family. To his honor it had to be said, even by his bitter enemies, that he never made a penny out of the great financial transactions which enriched so many others. He had established the credit of the United States on a sound basis and had enlisted the support of all propertied persons on behalf of the Federal government. Now he wanted to make some money for himself by his own private talents.

But he did not relinquish his hold on the government. He kept in constant correspondence with the officeholders, many of whom were in office by his favor, and his advice was followed by those of his own party with the strictest obedience. His prestige at this time was immense, amongst all those whose rank, property, influence or social position gave them something to say in political matters. The Federalists—now being called the "Hamiltonians" by many—were his personal possession.

When Washington retired from the presidency

after two terms of office, the Federalist candidate was John Adams. It is hard for us to imagine it now, but the parties did not really exist in those days: everybody was supposed to belong, more or less, to the same party. Some members of this general national party were on Hamilton's side, some on Jefferson's. George Washington had cherished the idea, in his noble simplicity, that the new nation could do without political parties. "If parties exist," he said serenely, "we must reconcile them."

He did reconcile them, to a considerable extent, for the whole eight years of his presidency, but no sooner had he gone home to Mount Vernon than the party strife broke forth more strongly than ever.

According to the cumbersome system of election at that time (soon to be changed), the person receiving the highest number of votes in the electoral college became president, and the person with the next highest number of votes became vice-president. Thus John Adams became the second president of the United States (1796) and Jefferson became his vice-president.

It was a troublesome, tiresome, dangerous four

years. Adams, a fussy and elderly man, suspicious of everybody, was a Federalist but was not under the thumb of Hamilton. Hamilton controlled all the members of Adams' cabinet and used to give them orders by private letter from New York, while Adams in Philadelphia knew nothing about it. The Federalists or Hamiltonians, the ruling party, became more and more pro-English, more and more determined to seize any opportunity to join England in war against France. The feeling of the people ran in the opposite direction for the most part, and the famous (or infamous) Alien and Sedition Laws were passed to keep public opinion in a strait jacket. These were two separate laws, often confused as one in the public mind. The Alien Law made it possible to deport any foreigner whose opinions displeased the established authorities. The Sedition Law enabled the established authorities to prosecute and imprison anybody who wrote, published or spoke in a manner opposing the official policy. Both laws were obviously unconstitutional but in a moment of hysteria they were accepted.

John Adams, who for all his fussiness had native shrewdness or even wisdom, never made use of the Alien Law, and his use of the Sedition Law was not as bad—as we see it now—as it seemed then. Some individuals suffered great injustice for their opinions. There were a good many arrests and several very notable imprisonments amongst newspaper editors. But each of these cases received so much attention, and aroused so much indignation, that it was a foregone conclusion that the acts would soon be repealed.

Before he finished his four years John Adams discovered that his cabinet was under Hamilton's control, and he summarily dismissed three of the principal members. The split that followed in the Federalist party was a sure guaranty that Jefferson's newly formed and organized party, calling itself the "Democratic-Republican" party, would win the election of 1800.

But for those four years, 1796-1800, Jefferson himself played a very quiet and unobtrusive part. He presided over the Senate with rigid impartiality, even when members were spending a large part of their time attacking him without naming him. (He is credited with having created most of the Senate rules which obtain to this day.) He did not try to go out into society because he knew that in the upper classes of Philadelphia he and his friends, known as "filthy Democrats," were not welcome. He encouraged his friends, who were innumerable, to form Democratic committees in every town, city and village in all the states, in preparation for the time when they would take over the power.

He continued to read, to study philosophy, to inspect rocks and fossils and plants and breeds of farm animals.

And strangely enough, when the time came, it was Alexander Hamilton, his firm and convinced opponent, who ensured the election of Thomas Jefferson to the presidency.

The way of it was this: under the strange and awkward system of election that still prevailed, although Jefferson was clearly the choice of the people in 1800, the electoral votes were even between him and Aaron Burr. Burr was supposedly of the same party as Jefferson (a "Democratic-Republican") but in fact he had played devious games with the Federalists and was strongly supported by a large section of that party.

The election therefore had to go to the House of Representatives, where the voting was by states.

There were fourteen states at the time. Jefferson carried eight of them on the first ballot and Burr six. Nine were necessary for the election.

This balloting took place at the Capitol on February 11th in a blinding snowstorm. The whole House fought its way up the hill—even one member who was brought in on a stretcher to cast his vote for Jefferson.

They stayed there and voted, ballot after ballot, all day and all night. At eight o'clock the following morning (February 12th) when after the twenty-seventh ballot there was still no change, the House adjourned until eleven o'clock the next day.

On the next day two ballots were taken without any change, and an adjournment was made until the following day (Saturday). Then three more ballots were taken with exactly the same results, and the House adjourned until Monday.

Meanwhile Burr was in Albany, saying nothing and doing nothing. He knew very well that his strength was coming from the opposing party—that to which he did not belong.

Hamilton was in New York in a steadily mounting rage. He detested Aaron Burr and regarded him as thoroughly unreliable, if not a downright traitor. He had always opposed Jefferson but he knew him to be an honorable man. Hamilton had defeated John Adams—had quite effectively ruled him out—but now he faced the possibility of seeing Aaron Burr in the presidency, and by the vote of the so-called Hamiltonians.

This was in many ways Hamilton's finest hour. He fought by every means in his power to ensure the election of Jefferson rather than of Burr. He wrote letters from morning to night, engaged in personal talks of persuasion, pleaded and threatened and implored. He no longer had control over his own Hamiltonians—who were, as a party, already falling apart, never to be put together again —but he did everything he could, and there were still some who would listen to him.

Meanwhile the crowds were getting ugly. They wanted Jefferson; the people in a great majority were on his side. When Monday passed without a decision it looked as if the new capital of Washington, into which the government had so recently moved, might be the scene of public rioting. The Hamiltonians had some hasty caucus meetings that night. On the next day, Tuesday, the State of

Vermont was allowed to change its vote from Burr to Jefferson, and the State of Maryland followed suit. Jefferson was elected.

It is hard now to imagine, when we see the great city of Washington, all concrete and marble and stone, what it was like at that time. The White House had been built, but neither furnished nor heated, and there were not even enough lamps to light it. Between it and the temporary Capitol was a sea of mud. The spaces were great, were even grandiose, but there were no pavements of any kind, no sidewalks or clear demarcations, no street lighting and even no efficient clearance of tree-stumps. Houses were like islands in the mud. If a man went to a friend's house for dinner he was obliged to remain all night because of the mud, the darkness and the unfamiliar geography. Anybody who ventured out at night was almost certain to get lost in the swamps, ravines and ruts of the vast mud hole.

When John Adams and his wife moved into the White House, Mrs. Adams, the thrifty Abigail, complained that it would take at least thirty servants to keep the house clean. None of the principal rooms of the house had been finished. She used the "great audience room" (what we call the East Room today) to hang up clothes to dry.

Georgetown, up on the hill, was an eighteenth century town with many comfortable houses of that period which remain even today, but it was much too far, on the wretched roads of that time, for the Congressmen and others who had business in the new capital. Nowadays it is no distance at all; then it was prohibitively far.

Congressmen lived in boarding houses as close as possible to the Capitol. Between the Capitol and the White House was the great mud sweep called Pennsylvania Avenue, bordered on either side by swamps which guaranteed chills and fever to anybody who dwelt there.

Jefferson lived during this whole drama of his contested election in Conrad's boarding house, near the Capitol. He always occupied the same place, at the foot of the long table where the other boarders had their meals. He never changed his place, never engaged in argument, and never seemed to be anxious over the outcome. He went to the Senate and presided over it with the same cold impartiality as before.

His correspondence shows that at this very time he was pursuing his usual interests. He wrote to a doctor friend, for example, of some bones which had recently been discovered that would be useful for the doctor's museum. Jefferson's coolness towards the political battle (it seems almost at times like contempt) was never more obvious. In one letter he says: "Which of the two will be elected, and whether neither, I deem perfectly problematical."

He was elected. But from then until his inauguration on March 4th, 1801, he continued to occupy his same seat at the foot of the boarding-house table, and declined better seats when they were offered him.

At four o'clock in the morning of March 4th John Adams left the White House in the dark and in a great hurry. He could not endure to remain for Jefferson's inauguration, to witness the triumph of a man who had, he said, "turned him out." They had been great friends in the heroic days of the Revolution, and afterwards in Paris; they were to become great friends again in their old age. At this moment Adams felt so sorry for himself that he was quite incapable of standing by Jefferson's side and watching him take the oath of office.

That morning at Conrad's boarding house up near the Capitol everybody was awakened by the thunder of artillery. Crowds poured into the village capital from all directions. The muddy streets were thronged. There was an informal national holiday, not proclaimed or authorized, but spontaneous, from Maine to Georgia. The demonstrations in all the cities and towns were such as had not been seen since the end of the Revolutionary war.

Democracy had conquered, and the instinct of the people knew it. The Alien and Sedition Laws would be repealed; there would be freedom of press and speech again; there would be an open ear for all petitions, all complaints and all grievances; Jefferson was pledged to repeal the direct taxes which had made the Hamiltonians unpopular; the people were to come into their own.

A military parade from the troops at Alexandria came up before Conrad's boarding house at ten o'clock in the morning. And Thomas Jefferson, very plainly dressed, came out of the boarding house and walked through the street to the Capitol to take the oath of office.

6 · *President Jefferson*

JEFFERSON'S INAUGURAL ADDRESS IS ONE OF the greatest appeals to national unity that have been made in our history. Only one or two of Lincoln's —his second inaugural in particular—have the same high, noble and generous tone towards enemies and friends alike.

"We are all Republicans," he said, "we are all Federalists."

This was said to two parties which had been engaged for almost twelve years—certainly for ten —in the most bitter strife ever seen in American political life.

And then—a famous passage:

"If there be any among us who would wish to dissolve this Union, or to change its Republican form, let them stand undisturbed as monuments of the safety with which error of opinion may be tolerated where reason is left free to combat it."

Some of Jefferson's own followers, the Republicans or Democratic-Republicans as they were called (ancestors of the Democrats of today), did not like this friendly and generous tone. Like so many politicians in every age, they wanted revenge on their opponents for the real or imagined injuries suffered when those opponents were in power. They wanted the spoils of office and they wanted those who disagreed with them somehow punished.

Jefferson, like Lincoln afterwards, disdained revenge. His object was to win as many as possible of the Federalists over to his side. He felt that the main stream of the American democratic tradition—a young tradition but a real one—was where he belonged and where many even of his opponents belonged. And as time passed he proved to be right: the Federalist party turned out to be "all head and no body," as he had once predicted it would, and a very large proportion of its voters turned to Jefferson. In his second election to the presidency, Jefferson won all but fourteen electoral votes out of the 176 then existing.

Jefferson's way of living was the first shock the "high society" folk (mostly Federalists) were to encounter. He disdained all ceremony, titles and rules of protocol or etiquette as they had been understood before. As we have seen, he walked to his inaugural, very plainly dressed and without guards or servants. He was determined to "republicanize" the government, to take away from it all those semi-monarchical and courtly forms which had obtained under Washington and Adams. (Washington cared no more for such things than Jefferson did, but he was strongly influenced by Hamilton and others who felt that the "dignity" of the presidency required stately ceremony.)

Jefferson made his own rules. He did most of his work in a ground-floor office where it was not his custom to dress up in formal clothing. Most of the time, like Lincoln, he wore carpet slippers. His clothing was always good, but he was careless of it. Callers, of whatever rank, were usually received in that ground-floor office, of which the principal feature was a mockingbird.

When the new British Minister, Mr. Anthony Merry, came to present his credentials, accompanied by the new Secretary of State, James Madison, President Jefferson was not in the state reception room to which they were conducted. Soon afterwards Jefferson appeared, from his office, in his ordinary clothes and in carpet slippers. Mr. Merry had dressed for the occasion in full court regalia with gold lace and a sword. Jefferson was extremely friendly, led the Minister to a chair and tried to talk to him in a courteous manner, but Mr. Merry had been deeply offended and never really got over it.

And worse was to come. The first time the British Minister and his wife, the redoubtable Mrs. Merry, dined at the White House, Jefferson's new system of etiquette came into play. He had decided that no ranks would be recognized in such merely social matters as seating at table, precedence through a door, etc., etc. The guests were to sit just wherever they happened to land, and in whatever company happened to be there.

The British Minister was purple with rage.

The British Minister and Mrs. Merry, who were exceedingly pompous people anyhow, were in full regalia that night, too. The Spanish Minister, Yrujo, was there with his beautiful American wife; so was the Secretary of State, Madison; so was the Secretary of the Treasury, Albert Gallatin, and the French Minister and his wife besides.

Jefferson was standing talking to James Madison's charming wife, Dolly, who for most of the time acted as hostess for the widower President.

Dinner was announced. Without thinking twice about it, Jefferson offered his arm to Dolly Madison and walked in to the dining room.

The British Minister was purple with rage. The President should have given his arm to Mrs. Merry. At least the Secretary of State should do so—but no! Madison was talking to Mrs. Gallatin at the time (wife of the Secretary of the Treasury) and he walked in to dinner with her. Finally there was nobody left in the drawing room but Mr. and Mrs. Merry, who were compelled to walk in to dinner last, and with each other.

The crowning blow to the Merry family came when they got into the dining room. Merry, the

Minister, thought he might console himself for all this rudeness by sitting beside Madame Yrujo, the lovely wife of the Spanish diplomat. But here again he was thwarted. A crude, rough fellow, some congressman unknown to diplomacy, thrust himself into the place His Excellency the British Minister had chosen.

The Merrys went home early and never really recovered from their indignation. They felt that His Majesty King George III had been insulted. Their complaints filled Washington and over-flowed to Philadelphia and New York. Some Federalist papers took it up as an example of the "vulgarity" of a democratic regime. Washington was sharply divided on the question, some of the fine ladies declaring that Jefferson's behavior was indefensible, and some saying that he had as much right to make his own rules of etiquette as the King of England or any other king.

But Merry made a long despatch to London about it, and according to his account his government was obliged to believe that some deliberate rudeness had been committed. Consequently James Monroe—Jefferson's other "pillar of happiness"

—who was then American Minister to England, was made to suffer a long series of slights and discourtesies which seriously interfered with his work as a diplomat.

Jefferson had never dreamed that his effort to democratize the White House could have such results. He had tried to make things as simple as possible, and to live as much as possible like any other citizen, without realizing that to many people simplicity in such matters is not at all desirable.

He wondered what to do, and in his candid mind there was but one thing: to ask the Merrys to dinner quite familiarly, without a large company, and get things explained. He asked Madison, Secretary of State, to find out if this would do.

Then Mr. Merry had his chance. He wrote a long rigmarole of a letter in which he declared that if he came to dinner at the White House as the official representative of His Majesty George III all the customary usages (i.e., rank, precedence and the rest) must be observed. It was his "duty to his Sovereign." And if he had been invited privately, not officially, it was his duty to refuse.

This was the meaning of the letter, although it

was wrapped in yards and yards of official language
and diplomatic sentences.

Jefferson dropped it. The British Minister and
his wife never appeared at the White House again.
Jefferson once said of her: "She is a virago who
has already disturbed our harmony extremely." In
difficult and dangerous times it was not at all convenient to have the British Minister on terms of
practical enmity with the White House, and this
was one result of Jefferson's democracy which
turned out rather badly.

But on the whole the new simplicities worked
well, the diplomats in general got used to them,
and although some American snobs regretted the
pomp and ceremony of Washington's and Adams'
day, the main lines of Jefferson's system have sur-
vived for a hundred and fifty years. That is, the
White House afterwards went back to regular sys-
tems of precedence for diplomats, but formality
and ceremony as such were reduced almost to zero
by Jefferson and have never been restored. What
ceremony is necessary and unavoidable is performed as simply as possible.

The Federalists—or rather their enraged leaders, who never could forgive Jefferson for being himself—took advantage of the feud with the Merrys to cultivate the friendship of the British Minister and in fact to conspire with him, on more than one occasion, against Jefferson's administration.

Jefferson was worried over the whole affair, even though he thought it to be a tempest in a teapot. After all, Monroe's business in London was important to the nation, and if Monroe was going to be snubbed and slighted at every turn he could not properly do his work. This was the awkward part.

But the feud never stopped until a few years later when the Merrys departed and the Erskines— David Montagu Erskine and his charming wife, born Frances Cadwallader of Philadelphia—came over to make all things amiable again.

One of the episodes of the long Merry-Jefferson feud shows that Martha Jefferson, the President's daughter (now Mrs. Randolph) was a chip off the old block. She did not come to Washington often because of the cares of her family in Virginia. When she did, for the first time, she received a solemn note from the British Minister's wife enquiring whether she was visiting the White House as the President's daughter or as the wife of a Virginia gentleman. If the first, Mrs. Merry would call upon her; if the second, Mrs. Merry would expect a call. Mrs. Randolph replied that she was indeed visiting the White House as the wife of a simple Virginia gentleman, but that, even so, she expected the first call, because in Jefferson's code of etiquette all strangers in the capital should be called on by all residents first.

It was one up to Mrs. Randolph. Mrs. Merry paid the first call.

Jefferson's first business as President and head of his party was to see that at least some of the government offices were held by persons of whose loyalty he could be sure. When he went to the White House there was not a Democrat on the government payroll. Every office, from the highest to the lowest, was held by a Federalist, a Hamiltonian. Most of these were bitterly hostile to Jefferson and to his party. Slowly, cautiously, and relying upon considerations of merit in every case, Jefferson began weeding out the least competent and loyal of the Federalists and replacing them by members of his own party. There was a tremendous uproar over this, and in many a history book Jefferson has been accused of inventing the "spoils system." ("To the victor belong the spoils"—a slogan of Jackson's time used to justify a wholesale turnover of government jobs when the administration changed.) There was no civil service then. But the proof of Jefferson's caution in this matter is that after his first administration was over fully half the government appointments were still held by Federalists, amongst them the bitterest enemies he possessed.

His own party, indeed, was sharply disappointed that he did not make a clean sweep of all his political enemies right away and supplant them with "deserving Democrats." His generosity and desire to conciliate the Federalists was thought, by some of his own friends and even by his loyal James Monroe, to be dangerous, as leading quite possibly to weakness. Jefferson proved right in the end, because by winning over large numbers of the rank and file of the Federalists to his side, he effectively destroyed that party, which soon afterwards disappeared from political life.

At the very beginning of his régime Jefferson declared (in his first Message to Congress) for an abolition of the unpopular direct taxes, for economies in the public service, reduction of the public debt, and an all-round paring down of the Hamiltonian system by which national debt helped create the nation. He was diligent to restore freedom of speech and assembly, impaired by the Sedition Act, and to pardon sufferers under that piece of unconstitutional legislation. And he attacked the highly illiberal Nationalization Act, which would have made it impossible to become an American in less than fourteen years' residence.

"Shall oppressed humanity find no asylum on this globe?" he asked.

All these measures proved highly popular and the angry Federalists could do nothing against them. Jefferson had a financial genius in his Secretary of the Treasury, Albert Gallatin, who actually was able to increase the revenue and abolish the internal taxation at the same time, with a steady yearly reduction of the public debt.

The Barbary pirates along the north shore of Africa, who had long been a thorn in Jefferson's flesh, were curbed by naval action, and the American merchant ships were the first in history who were allowed to pass through those regions without paying tribute to the Bey of Tripoli. (Even the French and the British found it more convenient to pay tribute than to go on fighting the pirates indefinitely.)

But the great event of Jefferson's first administration, and indeed one of the greatest events of all American history, was the Louisiana Purchase.

West of the Mississippi was the immense territory, of uncertain limits, which France had claimed by right of some very sketchy exploration. Where the Mississippi flowed into the Gulf of Mexico there was the established French colony of Louisiana, with the island of New Orleans. To the east of this, again with uncertain boundaries, was Spanish territory called "the Floridas," running along the Gulf through what is now the state of Mississippi. All these vast regions were the natural interest of the new and vigorous American nation, which was already steadily expanding westward.

Jefferson had had his eyes on the west since his youth, as we know. He was always vigilant to protect the rights of the westerners, the frontiersmen, whose products reached the world by way of the Mississippi river. When France ceded the huge Louisiana territory to Spain, it was provided that the Americans could continue to use the Mississippi and "deposit" their products for export at New Orleans. This "right of deposit," as it was called, was the lifeblood of the American West (all those states now called midwestern, such as Wisconsin, Illinois, Michigan, Indiana and Ohio).

The consternation was great in Washington when, at the beginning of 1803, it was learned that Spain had withdrawn this "right of deposit." The Mississippi was closed. Jefferson did his best with the Spaniards, but at this point an even worse blow fell. Spain ceded the whole immense territory, the greater part of what is now the United States, back to France.

Spain as a weak neighbor had been tolerable. France as a very powerful and dangerous neighbor, under the unconquered Napoleon Bonaparte, would be a very different problem, especially since the wars between France and England had become almost permanent.

The danger was bad enough with France alone; it was worse if France and England (then temporarily at peace) should again go to war and England might seize New Orleans or the Mississippi valley.

Jefferson acted as promptly as was possible in those days of slow sailing boats. He requested his minister to Paris, Livingston, to start talks with Napoleon and Napoleon's foreign minister, Talleyrand, for the possible purchase of the island of New Orleans and, if possible, the Floridas. The Floridas belonged to Spain, but it was obvious that if Napoleon wanted Spain to sell them, the deed would be done.

It never crossed Jefferson's mind, apparently, that Napoleon might under some circumstances be willing to sell the whole Louisiana territory, the great midriff of the North American continent.

There were conferences day and night in Washington with Madison and Monroe and Gallatin and others, over maps, figures, statistics and propositions. Jefferson decided to send his trouble-shooter, Monroe, to Paris to aid the regular minister in a negotiation with Napoleon. The danger of war between France and England was growing greater every day, and it was important to safeguard the Mississippi River before open hostilities began.

Monroe went. And by the time he got there the negotiation was already far advanced. War with England was now a certainty: Napoleon needed money. In addition, he had no certainty of being able to defend such huge territories at an immense distance from France, and he did not want to see them fall into English hands. He proposed (through Talleyrand) nothing less than the sale of the entire Louisiana territory, from New Orleans to the Rio Grande and up to Canada.

When Livingston asked the exact limits of the territory Talleyrand said: "You have made a noble bargain for yourselves, and I suppose you will make the most of it."

The old fox was suggesting that the Americans might push out the limits of the territory as much as they were able—and in fact, that is pretty much what the pioneers of the West did do after a while.

Monroe and Livingston were faced with a tremendous responsibility. They had no instructions to buy half a continent: they were supposed to buy the mouth of the Mississippi, the island of New Orleans. The price for the entire territory was only fifteen million dollars. (It is worth untold billions today.) It would take months to get new instructions from Washington. The two men drew a deep breath and signed the treaty of purchase.

When the news came to Jefferson he was startled: he had done far more than he intended. He had always known this negotiation was important. He had written to Monroe in Paris: "The future destinies of our country hang on the event of this negotiation." But this——!

And his conscience was troubled. He did not believe any president had the constitutional right to buy half a continent by a stroke of the pen. If he had been like Hamilton he could have argued that the treaty-making power "implied" the power to buy new lands—"implied powers" were what Hamilton relied upon for many transactions. But Jefferson had never believed in "implied powers": he always had wanted to stick to the exact letter of the Constitution.

Now, he thought, it was too late to go back on what his representatives had done in Paris, but he could ask for a constitutional amendment to make the whole business strictly legal.

While he was debating with himself, a new message came from Paris saying that if he did not make haste Napoleon might change his mind again.

Jefferson decided at once and submitted the treaty of purchase to the Senate. The Senate approved it by a vote of 26 to 5, and the House promptly voted the necessary funds by a vote of 90 to 25. Neither Senate nor House shared his scruples: both knew a bargain when they saw one.

No constitutional amendment was necessary and Jefferson was at last dissuaded from the idea that he should ask for one. The territory of the United States was increased one hundred and forty percent, and the richest continuous land empire in existence was laid open to the enterprise of the coming generations.

Jefferson's part in the Louisiana Purchase, like that of Monroe and Livingston, was highly justified. All had done the best they could for their country, and far better than anybody had dreamed at the beginning. But Napoleon's part was shady indeed. In selling the great country west of the

Mississippi he was violating a clause in his own constitution and also his solemn pledge to Spain that he would never give or sell Louisiana to a third power.

This, however, was not America's business: it concerned Napoleon's own conscience, which had already shown itself well able to get rid of paltry moral objections.

America took over the great new territory just seventeen days after the French governor had formally received it from the Spanish governor. What Europeans there were in the immense area were French and Spanish, with no experience of democracy. Jefferson decided to govern the territory for the time being by appointed officers, with the idea of forming new states out of it whenever that might be possible.

The birth of a great empire always excites the adventurous. Anybody who desired to better himself, for whatever reason—whether because he had failed at home, or because opportunities there were limited, or merely because the neighbors weren't friendly enough—wanted to go west and try his luck. As was only natural, there were both good and bad results for the human beings involved in

THE LOUISIANA PURCHASE

this great, sudden challenge to the enterprise of young America.

One very good result—an epic of the American story—is the Lewis and Clark Expedition, to the limits of the Louisiana Territory and beyond, to the very shores of the Pacific Ocean. This exploration, which had been in Jefferson's mind as a dream for years, was the first link between the Atlantic and the Pacific and fired all men's minds with the idea of the American continent as a whole.

Young Meriwether Lewis, described as "brilliant and elegant," was one of the interesting figures of Washington from the time he went there. A Virginian from Jefferson's own neighborhood (from Charlottesville), he became the President's private secretary at the age of twenty-six.

Jefferson liked and valued young Lewis, as he had Madison and Monroe at the same age. During the years when Lewis was his private secretary the President spent a good deal of time instructing him in how to carry out an expedition into the wilderness, what to look for, what to note down and what to bring back. Jefferson's interest in natural history and in agriculture predominated, as usual. He wanted to know what the soil was like, the climate, the rocks, the animals and the vegetation, how the rivers ran, how much waterfall there was, and what the arrangements of mountain and plain. Even before the Louisiana Purchase he had been training Meriwether Lewis in this way, always thinking of the West, the new and untrodden West where he believed America's destiny to lie.

The purchase of the greater part of the West made it natural to push forward the plans for the expedition. Jefferson worked it out himself in the greatest detail, as if he were personally going to lead it. In fact he tried to make his young secretary into a substitute for, or representation of, himself, doing the things he would have done if he had been able.

To lead the great expedition with him, Lewis chose, and Jefferson approved, Lieutenant William Clark, who had been a friend of Lewis' in army service. Towards the end of 1803, some months after the Louisiana Purchase, the two young men made their way to St. Louis and spent the winter near there, organizing their expedition and its recruits.

Their story is one of the romantic ones of American pioneering, repeated from generation to generation as an example of skill and courage. They started on May 14th, 1804, to ascend the Missouri River—a difficult feat—and by November second they had reached as far as what is now Bismarck, in North Dakota, where they passed the second winter in camp amidst the Mandan Indians. Early in April they started out again and pursued the Missouri upwards until it disappeared into three forks; then they followed one of these forks to a point in what is now Montana. There they abandoned river exploration and took to the mountains with some horses and a guide from the Shoshone Indians. After they had crossed the Rockies, they found a tributary of the Columbia and pursued their way until they reached the mouth of the Columbia, on the Pacific Ocean, November 15th. There they spent the third winter.

On the return trip they explored the Yellowstone; on September 23rd, 1806, they reached St. Louis again.

This daring and eminently successful expedition stirred the imagination of everybody in the United States. If a handful of hardy travelers could do it, so could anybody else: the westward limits were immensely far away and all that land and all its riches were there for the taking.

Lewis and Clark had gone over 8,000 miles from St. Louis to St. Louis.

Jefferson's delight with the results of their effort was great. Lewis brought him back some grizzly bears from the Rocky Mountains, and the President kept them in the White House garden, thus affording his enemies a chance to make fun of "Jefferson's bear garden." But serious scientific information of the first importance had been amassed, along with much that was new about the various Indian tribes, the soils and climates, the general nature of the new and unknown country. Nobody else had ever made the journey to the Pacific except much lower down, in the Spanish-Mexican zones.

Then, too, the opening up of the West evoked the ambitions of evil men. The classic example of this is Aaron Burr, who conceived the notion of cutting off the western territories from the United States and setting them up as an independent new empire, with himself as emperor.

Aaron Burr is one of the great puzzles of American history. He was clever to the point of real brilliance, but his scheme for the western empire was one of the stupidest and most scatterbrained enterprises it would be possible to imagine. He was at some point in his youth patriotic enough to deceive good judges, but when we read his personal letters now, long years afterwards, in all their naked cynicism, we get the idea that his patriotism was never anything more than a pose.

The truth probably is that the man was eaten alive by personal ambition, by the desire to make his own personal self, Aaron Burr, cock of the walk. When he found that this could not be done in the United States either in the Federalist party or in the Democratic party, he decided upon treason as a way out.

Burr had distinguished forebears and started life with every advantage. He was the son of the second president of Princeton—then called the College of New Jersey—and a grandson of the revered Jonathan Edwards, the colonial preacher. He fought in the Revolution with distinction (when he was only twenty) and was for a time on George Washington's staff, along with Hamilton and Lafayette. He commanded a regiment when he was twenty-one, a brigade when he was twenty-two. He left the army because of wounds, studied law and became for about ten years one of the most successful young lawyers in New York. His success and popularity were such that he had no trouble getting himself elected to the State Assembly and later to the United States Senate. In 1800, thanks to his influence in New York City, he was named on the Democratic-Republican ticket along with Thomas Jefferson and became Vice-President.

But Jefferson, the head of the Democratic party, never trusted him at all. During that deadlock which took place in February, 1801, Burr lent himself to every maneuver of the Federalist party, his supposed opponents, although Alexander Hamilton, the head of that party, distrusted him just as much as Jefferson did. Before he had finished his term as Vice-President, Aaron Burr was in such a peculiar position that nobody could be quite sure which of the two parties might claim his loyalty, if indeed he had any loyalty.

The man seems to have been without any moral standards at all, judging by the letters which have come down to us. He was perpetually on the brink of bankruptcy and burdened with debt, not through devotion to other things than money (as was the case with Jefferson and as was the case for years with Hamilton), but simply because he deliberately wished to defraud.

At the end of Jefferson's first administration it was impossible to keep Burr on as Vice-President. He was dropped, not only as Vice-President, but also as a member of the Democratic party. He then endeavored to get himself elected Governor of the State of New York, not as a Federalist exactly, but as an independent relying heavily on the angry Federalists (anti-Jeffersonians) for his support.

Hamilton raged, just as he had raged four years before. Hamilton knew that Burr was not to be trusted in any way, and it was a bitter thing to see that the Federalist party, Hamilton's own creation, was ready to support this man for Governor of New York. Hamilton's influence, plus Jefferson's from the other side, probably determined the result: Burr was defeated.

Then, nursing his wounds in the fury of a ruined gambler, a desperado, Aaron Burr decided that Hamilton had insulted his "honor." The only recourse was a fight to the death. Burr challenged Hamilton to a duel.

Hamilton's favorite son, Philip, had been killed in a duel four years before, and the sorrow had been the greatest of Hamilton's life. Perhaps for this reason, perhaps for some other, it seems that Hamilton had a feeling that he would be killed in the duel with Burr. Hamilton was calm and cheerful during the days that preceded the duel: Burr was busy practicing with his pistols. They both rowed across the river to Weehawken, in New Jersey—the classic dueling ground in those days, just where Hamilton's son had been killed—and took their places.

They were ten paces apart. Hamilton gave the signal to fire. Burr's first bullet killed him. Hamilton did not fire at all. This was July 11, 1804.

Dueling was not illegal, and Burr was not a murderer, but to all intents and purposes his career in the United States was over.

Then began his peculiar attempt to set up some kind of new state, colony or empire in the West. He had actually bought some land in Louisiana, perhaps with the idea of setting up a separate state of his own. But before he went west he had some interviews with the British Minister (our friend Mr. Merry, personally inimical to Jefferson) and with the Spanish Minister, Yrujo. The clearest evidence of treason is in the Royal Archives of Spain, and did not come to light for a century. There is no doubt that Burr wished to detach some part of the West from the United States, and was willing to take money and help from either England or Spain or both to do so.

He went west and had the luck to find a crazy Irishman named Blennerhassett, a man of some wealth, living on an island in the Ohio river. This Blennerhassett, bedazzled by Burr's conversation and the dream of a new empire, undertook to build boats and recruit men for the desperate enterprise.

Burr went on to the Mississippi where, after ups and downs in his conspiracy, he finally drew so much attention to himself that the government in Washington ordered his arrest. He was brought back to Richmond for trial, on charges of treason, and was acquitted because the actual treasonable acts (the building of the boats, the recruiting, the arming of the recruits) had taken place on Blennerhassett's island while Burr was absent.

He still had another treason trial coming up in Ohio, but jumped bail and fled to Europe. When he did return to America he eked out a long existence in obscurity, but the story of his wild ambition and his sensational fall from greatness has been a part of the American legend ever since.

Alexander Hamilton's death was also the death of the Federalist party. It disintegrated into a group of elderly rich men, mostly in New England, who no longer had any voters to support them, and whose whole endeavor turned into sundry attempts to break up the American Union. The first "secessionists" in our history, men who wished to take individual states out of our Union, were these New England Federalists. Hamilton would never have had anything to do with them and made it very plain before he died. Jefferson effectually destroyed them by the enormous size of his popular votes and thus erased them from the American record.

There is no doubt whatever that Jefferson disliked and distrusted Aaron Burr from the beginning. He did his best to get him convicted of treason, without, that is, interfering with the courts.

There is some doubt as to what Jefferson thought of Hamilton, or what Hamilton thought of Jefferson. They were enemies, yes. Between them they created the American political party system. Jefferson was the believer in democracy, Hamilton the believer in enlightened privilege. They fought each other for many years with every weapon they could command. Each had his hours or years of triumph. But when it came to a crisis, every single time, it turned out that Hamilton respected and trusted Jefferson and that Jefferson respected and trusted Hamilton. These two opposing geniuses, between whom the American governmental structure was built up, recognized greatness in each other.

Many years after Hamilton's death, when Jefferson was living at Monticello in retirement, a foreign visitor there was astonished to see two busts by an Italian sculptor against the opposite walls of the entrance hall of the house. One was of Hamilton, one of Jefferson. The foreign visitor expressed his surprise.

"Yes, you see," said old Jefferson, smiling, "opposite in death, as in life."

Thus the Louisiana Purchase, like every other event of the highest and greatest importance in human history, brought results without number, both good and bad. It called upon the heroism of the young and strong. It appealed to the romance of the far horizon, the dream of the restless boys who were to create America. It also appealed to the ambitions of the greedy, the ruthless and the men without scruple. Many things were to come of it, blood and toil, injustice and justice, aspiration, defeat and victory. The whole history of the country for another hundred years was to be largely—mostly—the story of how the West was conquered, whether it was to be slave or free, whether it was to participate equally in the government of the Union or go its own way. Jefferson had foreseen all this long before. It was his doing, essentially, more than that of any other man, just as the entire history of the country for a hundred and fifty years has been determined more by him than by any other man.

From the time of the Hamilton-Jefferson struggle, from the time of the Bill of Rights (the first ten amendments to our Constitution), from the time of the Lewis and Clark Expedition and the Aaron Burr conspiracy (two sides of the same coin), our course was determined. From that time on we faced west. And we faced west with no possible chance of anti-democratic or class government taking over the country. That was Jefferson's monumental achievement.

All the last part of Jefferson's second administration was embittered by the struggle between England and France. Jefferson's own sympathies had always been with France, even in times when it was necessary to be overindulgent toward French excesses. He was old enough to remember what a godsend the French help had been to the American people in their Revolution. Many of the younger men did not realize how difficult—or perhaps even impossible—it might have been to defeat the British army and fleet without French assistance. In addition, Jefferson had strongly felt the necessity of revolutionary reform in France. These sympathies had carried on even into the régime of Napoleon Bonaparte, an adventurous personal usurper who had no known right to do any of the things he did.

But Jefferson's sympathy with France disappeared altogether when the United States was in danger. Thus we find him writing to Livingston, when Louisiana was threatened by French occupation, that this disaster would throw the United States into England's arms.

"The day that France takes possession of New Orleans," Jefferson wrote, "fixes the sentence which is to restrain her forever within her low-water mark. It seals the union of two nations, who, in conjunction, can maintain exclusive possession of the ocean. From that moment we must marry ourselves to the British fleet and nation."

He, who had been known for decades as an opponent of British pretensions—particularly as regards the dominion of the seas—was ready at that moment to think of some kind of special and firm alliance with the old enemy, just in order to assure the freedom of the Mississippi River.

The British in those days thought it their right to stop any ship on the high seas, search it and seize anybody or anything they chose to seize on the ship. There was no recognized code which said how or why this should be done. It was simply done, because "Britannia rules the waves." Jefferson spent most of his eight years as president in protesting against this high-handed procedure. When England and France were at war the British interference with American commerce was practically total. No American ship dared sail unless it was able to prove that it had no goods aboard that might be going to France.

Jefferson, with Madison in the State Department and Monroe usually in Europe on ticklish assignments, spent the last years of his régime trying to keep out of war with both England and France, and at the same time trying to uphold the American right to sail the ocean and trade in freedom. It was an extremely difficult task and was not altogether successfully performed. War was avoided, but the freedom of the seas could not be ensured or guaranteed.

Jefferson ended up with an Embargo Act which kept all American shipping in port—blockading the blockaders, as it were. British commerce suffered a great deal, because even then the American states were the principal traders with the British Isles. But American commerce suffered too. The effects were mixed, and on the great question of the freedom of the seas, as on so many others, it is clear that Jefferson was far ahead of his time. It took a hundred and twenty years to bring about what he wanted to bring about in 1807 and 1808.

For three days he rode through a blinding snowstorm.

With all this, he had installed the Republic on a firmly republican and democratic foundation. Class rule, the rule of a few privileged persons, was forever afterwards impossible in the United States. The finances had been improved unbelievably—revenue increasing while taxes were lowered, the great miracle of all government—and the national debt had been greatly reduced. True, he had economized perhaps too much on Navy and Army, particularly the former, but it was in accordance with the best naval and military advice of the time. Freedom of speech and assembly were restored; the Bill of Rights was a reality.

He decided to leave the presidency at the end of his second term.

There was no necessity for him to do so. He was sixty-five years old and at the height of his intellectual powers. His party had practically swamped all other shades of opinion. His own power was acknowledged throughout the country. He could have had a third term with the greatest of ease—he was implored to accept it. But Jefferson did not believe that any one man should be president for too long. Two terms were enough.

When he made this clear, he reinforced the decision which had been taken by George Washington before him. As a result, two terms became the normal maximum for an American president, even though the Constitution made it possible for a man to be re-elected any number of times. The tradition of two terms was not to be broken until 1940, when, under the pressure of a menacing world situation, Franklin Delano Roosevelt campaigned for a third term and afterwards for a fourth. A constitutional amendment has since made it impossible for any man to serve more than two terms, the maximum which Jefferson considered wise for the Republic.

Jefferson left the White House for his beloved Monticello without a trace of regret. He had longed for retirement many times before and had been prevented from achieving it. He felt, he said, that nature had intended him for "the tranquil pursuits of science." It was only "the enormities of my times" that had forced him into politics, committing himself "to the boisterous ocean of political passions."

James Madison was to succeed him, with James

Monroe in attendance (shortly to become Secretary of State). There was a military parade for Madison's inauguration, but Jefferson escaped it by riding his own horse to the Capitol and tethering it to the palisades there. Thus he was able to wait for his faithful Madison, at the Capitol, as a private citizen.

There were farewell tributes to Jefferson all over the country. He spent a few more days in the White House, packing, while Madison and Dolly waited in their own house. He started out from Washington in a carriage, but the roads were so rough that for most of the time he rode horseback. There was a blinding snowstorm, just as on his honeymoon journey long years ago, and the old man rode through it with bent head for three whole days, his carriage following behind.

Down at the foot of the hill at Monticello—where there is now the entrance to the national shrine—Jefferson's daughter, grandchildren and many devoted Negroes were waiting for him. They walked home with him up the winding road, the private road.

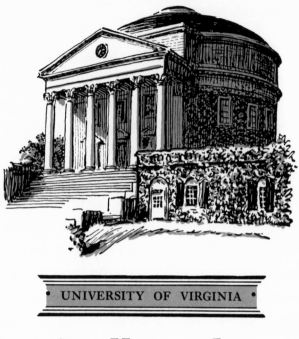

7 · *Home at Last*

THE EIGHTEEN YEARS OF JEFFERSON'S RETIRE-
ment were the golden sunset of a very great life.
Many active men are unhappy when they retire
from the battle. They waste away, fret over other
men's actions, and frequently develop ordinary
physical diseases which they never had (or never
noticed) while they were busy with public affairs.
We can all think of some examples of men who
have actually died from the maladies of retirement
—the boredom and nervousness of inaction.

Nothing of the kind happened to Jefferson. His last years were filled with the kind of activity he valued most—caring for his house and his crops, teaching carpentry and ironwork to his Negroes, maintaining a huge correspondence to all parts of the western world, watching over his brood of grandchildren, receiving an endless stream of visitors from Europe and all parts of America.

But most of all, his last years saw the fulfilment of one of his greatest dreams: the building of the University of Virginia.

Jefferson's passion for public education was as much a part of his nature as his passion for civil rights. From the very beginning he had evolved schemes aiming at what we have today, the free public education of all children as a function of the state. He was too far ahead of his times to get it adopted by the State of Virginia in the eighteenth century, but he never gave up. One of his recurrent dreams had been the creation of a real university in his beloved native state, and when he was able to do it he did it.

The noble buildings of the University of Virginia were his own work. He was not a professional architect, of course, and there may have been mistakes in his mathematics or in his engineering. But he was the first American who had the particular kind of building talent (and interest) which marks the real architect. He loved these buildings, as he loved the University itself, and to watch those stately red brick structures rising up, year after year, in nearby Charlottesville, all according to his own carefully elaborated plans, became his principal joy.

He had a telescope installed on the terrace behind his house at Monticello, and every day he could and did train the telescope on the University of Virginia in the valley below. If you go to Monticello today you will see the telescope and can look through it to the classic shapes of the college halls.

Jefferson valued the University of Virginia so highly that it was one of the three achievements he wanted inscribed on his tombstone: the Declaration of Independence, the Statute of Religious Freedom for the State of Virginia, and the University.

And then, of course, it is hardly common sense to call Jefferson's retirement by that name. It was not a retirement in the ordinary sense. True, he lived at home, where he had always wanted to be. But the whole world made a beaten path to his door. His activities were innumerable, and when you go to Monticello and see the gadgets he delighted in—the dumbwaiter, the storm windows, the clock calendar and all the rest of it—you will be well aware that this man never passed an idle day.

Moreover, he was in one sense just as powerful as ever in the affairs of the nation, because the next two presidents, Madison and Monroe, were the "pillars of happiness" upon whom he had counted all his life long. They remained devoted to him to the very end. Each was president for eight years, and each consulted Jefferson at every important point during those whole sixteen years. The president who succeeded Monroe, John Quincy Adams, who had started life as a Federalist and an opponent of Jefferson's, was converted to Jefferson's way of thinking early in the century and also came to power as a Jeffersonian. Thus, al-

Many visitors came to Monticello to see Jefferson.

though he was in "retirement," Jefferson actually had more influence on the presidents during these whole eighteen years than anybody else in the country.

Both Madison and Monroe got as close to Monticello as they could. Jefferson actually built Monroe's house for him—Ashlawn, it is called, and is in the immediate neighborhood of Monticello. Both Madison and Monroe visited Monticello as often as possible, and one room there is still called "Mr. Madison's room." These two men, so very different in appearance, character and manner, were united in their love for the old man. The brief period of a few years when they were jealous of each other soon faded away, and although they were opponents for the Democratic nomination in 1808, Madison, the winner, got Monroe into his cabinet as soon as it was possible, as Secretary of State.

Sometimes you will hear this sequence of great men (Jefferson-Madison-Monroe) referred to as "the Virginia dynasty." The expression was made up by enemies, but it has some truth in it. Madison and Monroe were like sons to Jefferson, the sons he never had. He was as proud of them as if they had been his own sons.

But what is perhaps a little more remarkable is that some others who were not at all of "the Virginia dynasty" had the same filial affection for Jefferson. The Adams family, for example, from generation to generation, had a genuine devotion to the old man of Monticello. John Adams himself, a cantankerous old man by all accounts, long a political enemy of Jefferson's, took many years to soften up, but deep down underneath he always had a tremendous regard for Jefferson, the friend of his youth.

Abigail Adams, his wife, had once taken care of Jefferson's younger daughter, Mary, when she first came over to Paris as a little girl. And in spite of the political enmity—very sharp in those days; enemies did not speak or write to each other— Abigail wrote Jefferson a warm letter of sympathy when Mary (Polly) died.

Then, years and years after both Adams and Jefferson had retired from Washington, John Adams broke out one night in Boston in the presence of several witnesses.

"I love Thomas Jefferson," he declared bellig-
erently, "and what's more, I always have loved
him."

This was speedily reported to Jefferson at
Monticello, and Jefferson instantly sat down and
wrote Adams a letter.

It was the beginning of the most interesting sus-
tained correspondence in American political history. Those letters make wonderful reading today.
The men were still political enemies, that is, they
belonged to opposing parties, but they had the
highest possible regard for each other and they had
the great foundation of common memories in the
struggle for freedom.

Adams, living chiefly in his library, had much
more time to write letters than Jefferson did.
Sometimes, therefore, Adams would write two or
three letters to Jefferson's one. Age had mellowed
Adams enormously. Time was when he would
have taken offense if a letter of his were not answered at once. Now he no longer cared about such
things. Once Jefferson had been off for several
days, riding around the outlying parts of his estate,
and during this time no less than three letters

from Adams accumulated. Jefferson was very apologetic about this, but the old man in Massachusetts didn't mind. He said he was willing to write any number of letters to Jefferson's one.

"It is important," he said, "that we two should live long enough to understand each other."

They discussed everything imaginable, philosophical ideas, natural history, agriculture, the quality of American democracy, the events of the day, international relations, ancient history, characters known to both—a vast range of subjects—and always with perfect courtesy and good humor. It is quite clear that the mutual regard between these two giants of the new world was keen and high. Adams was not always a person for whom one could feel any warmth of affection during his public career, but in his retirement he shows up as a wonderfully intelligent, cultivated, brave and wise old man.

There was one dark shadow in Jefferson's golden sunset. That was money. He never had been very economical. When he was Minister to Paris he spent far more money on his house, and particularly on food and wine, than the Congress would ever pay back. During his eight years in the White House, although he disdained pomp and ceremony, he kept the best table that had ever been seen in Washington. Even his bitterest enemies were delighted to dine with him because of the food and drink as well as because of the conversation.

Now, at Monticello, he simply kept open house for eighteen years. Anybody who wanted to come there was welcome, and the house was never empty. This meant huge meals—they ate far more in those days than we do now—and a vast consumption of the best French wines. Those meals contained three or four meat courses, for instance (ham and chicken and roast veal or roast beef) as well as all the courses that came before and afterwards. The punch bowl in the hall was kept filled all the time. A guest might arrive with a carriage, horses and perhaps two slaves, a personal servant and a coachman, and stay a month or two months or even three. Jefferson was always happy to see anybody who came, stranger or old friend.

This kind of thing, along with a certain carelessness about giving money away, made heavy inroads on Jefferson's once large income. He spent a great deal of money on the house itself, and nobody knows exactly how much he gave away to the University of Virginia and other generosities. As a result he had to start selling his beloved land, bit by bit, in order to keep on going in the lordly style which was his custom.

When you go to Monticello you will see how carefully the books were kept. Every bit of bacon that was sold, every pound of tobacco, was carefully entered in the books in that wonderful copperplate writing which was characteristic of the time. It looks, from the bookkeeping, as if everything on the estate were economically ordered.

And yet the perpetual open house, the endless expenditure on building, on gardens, on plants and trees and horses and household gadgets, came in the end to weigh so heavily that Jefferson was practically bankrupt. At the end of his life (just two years before he died) the nation was horrified to learn that the old man had run through his whole fortune and estate. It was reported that he would have to sell Monticello in order to pay his debts. A subscription was taken up amongst patriotic citizens, and some $20,000 resulted as a gift to Jefferson so that he could live out his days in his own house. But as soon as he was dead the house had to be sold, with all its furnishings and valuable objects, in order to satisfy his creditors.

The same was true of his slaves. He had owned a hundred and fifty slaves at one time, and never did approve of the sale of human beings. He freed a considerable number of his slaves by his last will and testament, and no doubt wished to free them all but was held back by the thought of his debts.

The money troubles were not enough, even so, to impair Jefferson's serene and noble spirit. He had never paid a great deal of attention to his own money, although as president he had carried out the most economical administration known to our history. The truth is that Jefferson, the most convinced and dedicated believer in democracy we have produced, was himself an aristocrat by nature and temperament. He thought, felt and spoke like an aristocrat. All his life long he simply assumed that there would be enough of everything, that he did not have to worry about such

Lafayette visited Jefferson at Monticello.

things, and that it was only right and proper that his house should be open to all comers.

In personal manners he was democracy itself. In or out of the White House, he treated all people alike. He said himself that he could not feel any difference of status between people: that a king and a poor farmer were the same to him. He proved this abundantly. But at the same time he would not dream of putting any but the costliest and best French wines on his table.

Toward the end of his days the Marquis de Lafayette came to America and made his pilgrimage to Monticello. Jefferson was eighty-three; Lafayette was thirteen years younger. When the legendary Frenchman, the friend of old, tottered on to the terrace behind Monticello, Jefferson was standing by his telescope looking, as so often, at his University. He turned and made his way feebly toward Lafayette. They embraced each other and wept. Both were too old to talk of much except memories.

But the strangest relationship of all was that between John Adams and Jefferson. They were the only survivors of the great days; all the others had gone; they clung to each other, at a distance, by means of their extraordinary correspondence.

And when it came time for them to go, too, they departed this life on the very same day. It was the Fourth of July, 1826, the fiftieth anniversary of that Declaration of Independence which, although Jefferson wrote it, had been to some extent a product of both their minds.

Adams' last words were: "Thomas Jefferson still lives."

It is difficult to state the full extent of our debt to Jefferson. We owe to him not only the Declaration of Independence and the Bill of Rights, the democratic form of our history and the principles of freedom in equality, the dollar itself, the concept of religious freedom, the great idea that the slaves should be free, but also in the simplest practical sense, the immense extension of our territory and the discovery of the West. It would be impossible to maintain that any other American, even Abraham Lincoln, did more for his country and his people.

And Lincoln, too—although he was the head of another party, descended directly from the Hamiltonians—acknowledged his debt to Jefferson as being the greatest of all. He declared that he had never had a political thought or feeling which did not find its origin in the Declaration of Independence.

"If we want a sure proof of Thomas Jefferson's greatness," said Lincoln, "it will be found in the fact that men of every variety of political opinion, however far asunder, find confirmation of their doctrine in him. Every party in this country today reckons Jefferson as its patron saint."

It was Lincoln who had to carry on Jefferson's uncompleted work and abolish slavery in our states, something Jefferson would have done very early if it had been allowed.

Jefferson's life was one of those in which we find larger truths forever indicated, and in a very true sense our entire history could be outlined from the content of his ideas. Our public school system today, to take a fundamental example, is very much what he would have created if he had been able to do so. The whole of the golden West, upon which the American story has been largely built, was the child of his far-sighted imagination. At every turn we have to give thanks to the genius of that great Virginian, who understood so much, strove so valiantly and spoke for the best that there is in us at the very dawn of our existence.

Index